LIBRARY OF ART

PUBLISHER - DIRECTOR: GEORGE RAYAS

THOMAS HOPE
(1769~1831)

PICTURES FROM
18ᵀᴴ CENTURY
GREECE

BENAKI MUSEUM ❀ THE BRITISH COUNCIL ❀ PUBLISHING HOUSE «MELISSA»

PUBLISHER: "MELISSA"
10, Navarinou str., 10680, Athens, tel. 3600865

Editorial Supervisor: LAMBRINI VAYENA-PAPAIOANNOU

Artistic Supervisor: RACHEL MISDRAHI-CAPON

Special photography: MAKIS SKIADARESIS

Printed by "MELISSA" in Greece, 1985

Colour separation by MELISSA'S photo lab.

Photo-typesetting by PHOTOSYN, N. MAVROMMATIS and Co Ltd

THOMAS HOPE
(1769~1831)

PICTURES FROM 18TH CENTURY GREECE

TEXTS: Fani-Maria Tsigakou

CONTENTS

PREFACE

This publication is the result of a combination of strong though invisible links. Those, on the one hand, who are interested in artistic problems of the classical world, will consider it as the expression of an intellectual affinity with Thomas Hope: a misty and romantic personality. They will also consider it as a vision of classsical antiquity inspired by the sensitivity prevalent at the end of the 18th century, long before any scientific approach to the study of classical archaeology had been conceived and developed in Europe. Those, on the other hand, who examine the visual impressions of Thomas Hope which resulted from his Greek tour and who try to visualise and reconstruct a more recent picture of the Greek world, will discover some even more fundamental blood ties. They will discover these through contemplation of the new aspect of Greece and her superb natural scenery, the charm of her architectural forms, the warmth of her human relationships and the intimacy that is revealed through Hope's recording of the people. They will sense finally the evocation of the ethos of the period which preceeded the saga of the Greek War of Independence.

Memories of classical values have been transformed into the concept of our duty to understand ourselves and into a sense of responsibility for revealing the treasures burried in our museums to their rightful owners.

However, a decisive element in the publishing of this book was the role played by factors of another kind: the sense of responsibility which is displayed by the educational policy of the Benaki Museum itself, towards both scientific research and the public at large; deep respect for the author of the text; the long standing relationship with the publisher; and solid friendship for the photographer whose admirable sensitivity has enabled him to render truthfully the design and colours of these works of art.

Finally, I will refer to the close relationship between the British Council and the Benaki Museum, which dates from 1974, when we undertook an exhibition of Byron's contribution to poetry. The fact that the British Council happens to be celebrating the 50th Anniversary of its contribution to the intellectual life of this country is a splendid coincidence. Indeed, it is most encouraging to confirm, once more, that the restrictions of space and time are irrelevant to cultural matters.

ANGELOS DELIVORRIAS, Director, Benaki Museum

Although not British-born, Thomas Hope adopted Britain from the age of 26 until he died aged 62. Britain in turn adopted him as she had adopted Van Dyck, Rubens, Kneller, Lely, Zoffany, Hollar and Holbein. The fact that Hope's work in the British Museum is kept in the British Collection is proof enough of that adoption. In his book 'Thomas Hope and the Neo-Classical Idea' (John Murray, 1968) Dr David Watkin has drawn attention to the influence which Hope had on British taste in architecture and design. From these early and hitherto unpublished sketches made during his visits to Greece and Asia Minor we obtain a fascinating insight into what influenced him. His passion for meticulous detail was already well developed and as a result these pages offer much to the student of Greek architecture, costume and customs at the end of the eighteenth century.

1984 is the 50th anniversary of the creation of the British Council and we are delighted to be able to commemorate the event in Greece in a way which we hope will be of lasting scholarly value. The seed of the idea for a joint publication with the Benaki Museum to mark the occasion was first planted in my mind by my colleague Kenneth Whitty whose apparently random assassination on 28 March 1984 appalled all right-minded people. He in turn had caught the enthusiasm of Fani-Maria Tsigakou of the Benaki Museum, a former British Council scholar and author of the excellent book 'The Rediscovery of Greece' (Thames and Hudson, 1981).

In our collaboration with that distinguished Greek institution the Benaki Museum we also see a symbol of the wider cooperative relationship between Britain and Greece in the sphere of art and ideas.

I should like to thank most warmly the Trustees of the Benaki Museum, the Director, Dr Angelos Delivorrias, his technical colleagues and, of course, Fani-Maria Tsigakou herself for their unfailing and creative help in this venture.

PETER NAYLOR
Representative, British Council, Greece

INTRODUCTION

Museum objects have their personal history; that adds to their charm. The history of the Hope collection - on its way to the Benaki Museum - began half a century ago:

"September 22nd, 1930

Messrs B. T. Batsford, Ltd
94, High Holborn
London, W.C.1

Dear Sirs,
Out Minister Mr Caclamanos has written to inform me that you have a collection of drawings by Thos. Hope, for which you are asking £120.
As I am interested in this collection and would like to acquire it, if possible, for the Nation, would you kindly give me all the information you can on the subject, informing me at the same time whether you could see your way to make a reduction in the price, which I cannot help thinking rather high.
Thanking you in anticipation.

Yours truly.
Antonis Benakis"

This is the first of a series of letters that was exchanged between Antonis Benakis and B.T. Batsford in relation to the purchase of the Thomas Hope drawings. In Benaki's last letter, dated November 8th 1930, we read:

"Dear Sirs,

I thank you for your letter of October 28th, giving me all the details of Thomas Hope, and informing me that the drawings are his original ones.

Much as I am interested in this lot, I very much regret I cannot, for the time being at least, buy it at the price".

In David Watkin's most interesting study entitled *Thomas Hope and the Neo-Classical Idea* which was published in 1968, the author mentions (on p. 277): "These volumes of drawings [made by Hope on his travels between 1787 and 1795... of which the vast bulk depict life, landscape and costume in Turkey, Asia Minor, Syria, Egypt and Greece] appeared in Christie's Deepdene Library Catalogue 1917, Lots 395-7, but, it seems, had been withdrawn before the sale took place. They next turned up in an undated Sale Catalogue (c. 1930) of 100 *Old Rare or Unique Illustrated Books, Collections of Original Drawings, Designs, Engravings, etc... offered for Sale by B. T. Batsford Ltd.* B. H. Blackwell Ltd, to whom Batsford's Antiquarian Department has passed, inform me that they believe the volumes were sold to "the Chicago Art Museum". Enquiry and advertisement in Chicago and elsewhere in America has not so far resulted in the discovery of these drawings".

In 1977, during the course of general re-organization of the Benaki Museum's Library, five volumes of about 350 - unsigned - drawings were discovered. The folio-size volumes are bound in full contemporary brown russia, gilt tooled. Two of the volumes are

1. A FOUNTAIN OF CONSTANTINOPLE

Pen and sepia drawing on paper 41×53.5 cm. Inv. No 27354. Inscribed: "Side view of the Fountain before the outer Gate of the Seraglio".

inscribed on the spine: DRAWINGS BY T. HOPE; these and a third one display the Hope family's motto and arms embossed with gilt on both covers. The arms together with other decorative details show the globe with a small part missing, while a Latin inscription that runs around it reads: AT SPES NON FRACTA. This is a play on words referring to the Hope family name: (SPES = Hope). Upon examining the volumes we realised that their contents fully coincided with the description given in the Batsford Sale Catalogue (c. 1930) which is mentioned by Watkin. Moreover, a pen-drawing of a "View of the Seraglio" included in one of the volumes, (ill. 7), is identical to the one illustrated in D. Watkin's book, in pl. 17. The description given in the Batsford Sale Catalogue is as follows: "Lot 397. Vol I comprises 66 drawings on 33 leaves, mostly in pen and sepia ink, but a few in wash or tinted, of architecture and peasant life in Hungary and the Balkans; Roman remains in the Balkans; ancient remains on the Bosphorous; Byzantine churches and monuments in Constantinople; the great mosques of Constantinople; Islamic architecture and details of decoration in Constantinople and Asia Minor; Islamic and Byzantine tombs; Turkish palaces, etc.; with a few plans. *Folio* (15 by 20 in.).

Vol II comprises 121 drawings in pen and sepia ink, on 33 leaves, of Turkish palaces in Constantinople, with details of ceilings, grilles, etc.; Turkish state barges and pleasure-boats; Turkish court, everyday and military dress, with turbans, head-dresses, etc.; streets and squares in Constantinople; Alexandrian and Hellenistic ruins, friezes, reliefs, etc.; Greek costume, peasant groups, dancers, etc.; Greek towns and ruined temples; and coastline landscapes in Greece. *Folio* (15 by 20 in.).

Vol III comprises 71 drawings in pen and sepia ink, on 33 leaves, of landscapes, town views, ancient remains, reconstructions, plans, etc., in Greece, including Hydra, Mycenae with its treasuries, Athens, Antiphellus, etc.; Greek and Albanian costume; sepulchral monuments at Jerusalem; Syrian, Bedouin and Egyptian costume, turbans, headdresses, peasant types, etc.; Nile craft; and the catacombs of Alexandria. *Folio* (15 by 20 in.).

Lot 395. Vol IV contains 150 drawings and sketches in pen and ink, pencil, wash and colour, mounted on 106 leaves. This is a more heterogeneous collection than the contents of the preceding volumes, ranging from quite rough and unfinished sketches to highly finished and beautifully coloured drawings; and, by the variety of techniques displayed, it is probable that a few are by other hands than Hope's. One or two prints and engravings are also included. The subjects comprise sketch-views and large, folding panoramas of Constantinople and the Golden Horn; plans, details and interiors of the Sultan's Palace; Turkish inscriptions; a fine, coloured drawing of a Turkish pavilion, with coloured plans and sections; sketches and panoramas of Ephesus, Delos, etc.; ruined Greek temples, capitals and sculpture, including a series of Aegina, with maps and plans, Corinth and Athens with its streets and monuments; types of Aegean craft, and a series of sketches of Egyptian landscapes, mosques, palaces, interiors, friezes, reliefs, architectural details, etc., with the Sphinx and the Pyramids, remains of ancient temples,

2. A ROOM IN A TURKISH PALACE

Sepia and watercolour drawing on paper 20×29 cm. Inv. No 27368. Inscribed: "Room in a Turkish palace".

Room in a Turkish palace.

53

3. A RECEPTION ROOM OF THE SUMMER PALACE IN CONSTANTINOPLE

Pen and watercolour drawing on paper 19×29 cm. Inv. No 27367. Inscribed: "Salon of the Sultan Valide in the Summer Seraglio".

peasant groups, camels, etc. The volume is lettered on the back "Egyptian Drawings". *Folio* (13 1/2 by 19 1/2 in.).

Lot 396. Vol V which is of considerably larger format, contains 117 drawings on 62 leaves, of large, minutely detailed pencil panoramas of Turkish and Greek landscapes, including Constantinople with various palaces and citadels on the Bosphorus, Mount Athos, Alexandria in Troas, Antiparos, Nauplia, Palamidi, etc.; also Tyre, Jerusalem, Alexandria and Gizeh. Then follows a series of beautifully finished wash drawings of bridges, aqueducts, monuments, the ancient walls, mosques, palaces, landscapes etc., in the vicinity of Contantinople; views of Alexandria in Troas, Paros, Tinos, Hydra, Mycenae, etc.; and drawings and details of mosques and palaces in Constantinople and Turkey, based on rough sketches appearing in earlier volumes of the collection. *Large Folio* (18 by 26 in.).

Bound in full contemporary brown russia, gilt tooled (vols I, II and III in Hope's library binding, with his crest on the side; the remaining volumes in a practically identical binding but without the crest) c. 1787-1795. From the Deepdene Collection. An absolutely unique item".

A sixth volume containing sketches for Hope's publication entitled *The Costume of the Ancients* was also included in that sale catalogue, with the following description:

Lot 315. Vol VI, a much smaller volume lettered "Outlines for my costume", consists of a collection of sketches and studies made by Hope for his *Costume of the Ancients* published in 1809. It contains 109 mounted drawings of ancient Greek and Roman costume, with a few Egyptian and Assyrian examples, including male and female dress, armour, helmets, drapery, head-dresses and coiffures, peasant dress, dancers' dress and specimens of ancient furniture and decoration. 4to (9 1/2 by 11 1/2 in)".

This volume is now deposited at the Gennadeios Library in Athens[1] where it was bequeathed by the Greek collector Damianos Kyriazis. In fact, when checking the provenance of the Benaki Library volumes, we found out that three out of the five volumes of drawings came from the Kyriazis bequest. We may therefore assume that Damianos Kyriazis (1890 - 1949), a prominent Greek collector and a close friend of Antonis Benakis bought part of the set, so that the two friends could share the expense. And it is thanks to this happy co-operation that one of the earliest visual documents revealing aspects of Greek landscape and life can now be studied and enjoyed by visitors to the Benaki Museum.

Thomas Hope was born in Amsterdam in 1769, of a prosperous banking family of Scots who had settled in Holland towards the end of the seventeenth century. His father, John Hope (1737-84), had married in 1764 the daughter of the Burgomaster of Rotterdam, Philipinna van der Hoeven (1738-90) and they had three sons, Thomas, Adrian-Elias and Henry Philip. Having achieved a remarkable position as aristocrats of commerce, the Hopes were equally established as distinguished art-collectors and patrons.

Upon reaching his eighteenth birthday Thomas set out on the Grand Tour as any other young man of his rank. However, his

4. GREEK VILLAS ON THE BOSPHORUS

Pencil and sepia drawing on paper 19.5×29 cm. Inv. No 27338. Inscribed: "Greek villas and quay on the Bosphorus".

5. A SCENE IN BUCHAREST

Sepia and watercolour drawing on paper 39.5×54 cm. Inv. No 27353. Inscribed: "Church of St Sava, and Tower built by Charles XII at Bucharest seen from the cortile of the Prince's winter Palace".

journeys were more extended and remarkably longer since they lasted eight years, from 1787 up to 1795. Before the end of the eighteenth century Thomas Hope had made successive visits to Italy, Spain, France, Greece, Egypt and the Middle East.

In 1795 the Hopes had settled in London having fled Holland on the arrival of the Napoleonic armies. His parents dead and himself heir to a substantial portion of the Hope fortune, Thomas set out to launch himself into English upper class society. In 1799 he acquired a grand town mansion built by Robert Adam in Duchess Street and in 1807, a year after his marriage to Louisa Beresford, he bought the country house and estate of Deepdene in Surrey. The purpose of both mansions was not only to entertain, in the most extravagant manner, fashionable English society but also to accommodate his numerous collections within a dazzling and distinct setting which expressed the owner's novel aesthetic considerations, the so-called Hope style.

Undoubtedly, in both range and quality the Hope collections rivalled those of a museum. From the age of twenty Hope's precocious talent as a connoisseur had been manifested through the acquisition of two exquisite pieces of antique sculpture which he found in Rome. Within a few years his collection of antiquities grew spectacularly; in 1801 he acquired two-thirds of the Hamilton vases which were sold at Christie's, while five years later his collection of vases amounted to 1500. The various collections of Greek, Roman and Egyptian antiquities were to be seen in the new wings that were created at Duchess Street, and fine specimens of old master paintings were displayed in specially arranged rooms, such as the "Picture Gallery" and the "Flemish Picture Gallery".

Hope's sensibility as a patron of contemporary artists led him to single out - while he was still in his twenties - such artists as John Flaxman, for whose works a new room was specially designed in the Duchess Street mansion, and Bertel Thorvaldsen who executed a complete set of busts for the Hope family. It was Hope who bought Benjamin Haydon's first canvas which was exhibited at the R.A. in 1807. And it was Hope's militant pamphlet, entitled *Observations on the Plans... for Downing College,* which was written in 1804 in support of the revolutionary design submitted by the then unknown architect William Wilkins, that led him to confront a whole body of Royal Academicians.

Although Hope's pronouncements on architecture and art did not facilitate his standing with some eminent authorities within the artistic establishment, he did succeed in becoming a distinguished public figure who was regarded with respect and who was able to exercise considerable influence over the cultural world of his time. His active involvement with a great number of artistic societies is characteristic. Furthermore, his engagement in such spheres of influence provided him with an excellent opportunity of propagating his individual aesthetic. Indeed, Hope's style, a synthesis of a variety of models inspired by a composite vision of ancient civilisations, helped shape Regency taste. Moreover, his open appraisal of Greek architecture and his zeal for hellenistic ideals created the breeding-ground for the Greek Revival. Hope's concern for the establishment of authentic Greek architecture which had been manifested in 1804 was followed by a further propagation of ancient Greek models into contemporary life through a series of publications such as: *Household Furniture and Interior Decoration,* in 1807; *Costume of the Ancients,* 2 vols, in 1809 and *Designs of Modern Costume,* in 1812. Their illustrations, after Hope's drawings, were based upon close observation of antique prototypes taken from the painted scenes on Greek vases, a great many of which were to be found in his private collection. These plates, some of which were based on actual specimens which were displayed in his house, reinforced the archaeological tendency in Regency interior decoration. Additionally they provided the reader with a convenient and simple vocabulary of costume and interior decoration *à l'antique.*

Hope was not only able to put his theories into practice by creating sumptuous interiors adorned with original pieces of furniture, but he also succeeded in popularising his aesthetic through these illustrated publications which could be considered as manuals of the Hope style.

Hope's talent for re-creating the atmosphere of remote civilisations and places revealed yet another capacity, that of a writer of a highly acclaimed romantic novel which he published anonymously in 1819 under the title *Anastasius or the Memoirs of a Modern Greek written at the close of the 18th Century.* In a three-volume, dramatic story of a young Chiot who runs away to sea after misbehaving with the daughter of his father's chief and until his death goes through legendary adventures in various countries around the Mediterran-

6. JERUSALEM, VIEW WITH THE "MOSQUE ON THE ROCK"
Pen and sepia drawing on paper 39×54 cm. Inv. No 27380. Inscribed: "Mosque in the site of Solomon's temple at Jerusalem".

ean and Middle East, Hope revives settings and manners of the eastern lands he had known in the course of his travels. " *[I]* was in every other place which I describe minutely in Anastasius", Hope once wrote[2] and indeed, one must take his word for it, especially after one has been through the visual records of his travels which are now preserved at the Benaki Museum.

Hope visited Greece twice: first during his Grand Tour of 1787-95, and secondly towards the end of 1799. It was during his second visit that he made a tour of the Morea in the company of Procopio Macri, the Levant Company's Consular Agent in Athens and the father of Teresa, Byron's "Maid of Athens". It seems that in order to have in his possession a more complete portofolio of Greek views Hope also acquired works other than his own. He employed, for example, the French artist Michel François Préault who had previously been in the service of Procopio Macri as well as of the English traveller John Tweddell. Hope made equal use of the Greek works of the French Consul Louis Sebastien Fauvel, such as pls 64-65 which are included in vol IV[3]. I believe that the *View of Scaros* (pl.88) must be attributed to Fauvel as there are great similarities in the handling of the pen as well as in the lettering. The pencil sketch of *The Capucin Monastery* (pl. 34) must also be in Fauvel's hand; the title is inscribed by Hope but that could have been added later. Hope borrowed and copied from Fauvel: some of the archaeological plans of Athens which the French Consul had based on his researches are depicted in pls 20, 22-23, annotated afresh by Hope according to his own readings of ancient writers and his own observations. In his views of the *Monument of Salamis* (pl.100) and of *Corinth* (pl.42), Hope mentions that these were copies after Fauvel. The notes written on the drawings provide us with a multitude of historical information about the subject depicted. Hope quotes briefly earlier travellers, often with the aim of criticising their opinions. His general tone of confidence when dealing either with problems of identification of classical sites or with attributions of ancient monuments is typical of that of the erudite Grand Tourist.

Thomas Hope's collection of drawings is of multiple importance: not only does it contribute towards the authentication of his descriptions of his travels and demonstrates his skill in draughtsmanship, but this large body of work also contributes towards our knowledge of Greek scenery, costumes and architecture in the late eighteenth century. Greece has been fortunate in that she has had her "portraitists": the foreign travellers who explored the land and recorded its sites and people. Any Greek subjects that can be traced among the works of foreign artist-travellers are highly treasured by modern scholars essentially because they constitute the only visual reference to the image of Greece in the centuries of Franco-Turkish domination. Undoubtedly, the Greek historical scene has not always been rendered with scholarly correctness by painters or by writers. This is but natural since, however authentic these Greek subjects might seem, they are in fact equally revealing of the artist's prejudices and his traditional liabilities; their documentary value, therefore, relies essentially upon the artist's intellectual agility and adaptability, that is, his ability to identify with the specific cultural and historical area to which he is introduced. Luckily enough, in Hope's case, we are presented with a more scientific approach because his works in the Benaki Museum collection are free from either selective eliminations or emotional confusions. Moreover, we should not disregard the fact that they were executed at the close of the eighteenth century, that is, before Greece had become a fashionable subject-matter for artists of all nationalities. Hope's faithful and accurate representations add much to our historical knowledge of Greece, for indeed his descriptive line has captured and retained every feature in the landscape he drew, emphasizing each architectural detail.

In the Greek drawings that are presented here, Hope's technical efficiency is evident, combined with skill in perspective and a fine sense of composition. Above all, the works testify to his superb draughtsmanship. Hope's fine and sensitive pen outline provides strong evidence of a natural facility rather than of a professionally acquired skill. "I scarce was able to hold a pencil, when, instead of flowers, landscapes... of which the imitation chiefly delights the generality of such children as shew a turn for the arts of design, I already began dealing in straight lines", he confessed in 1804[4]. Indeed, the Greek drawings show him as a brilliant draughtsman with a great power of selecting what was most relevant in form and texture.

Hope's depictions of costumes are remarkable for their authenticity and detailed observation. Certainly, this is hardly surprising for the author and illustrator of *Costume of the Ancients* and *Designs*

7. A PARTIAL VIEW OF CONSTANTINOPLE
Sepia drawing on paper 26×34.5 cm. Inv. No 27187. Insctibed: "View of the Seraglio point as seen from my window at Pera".

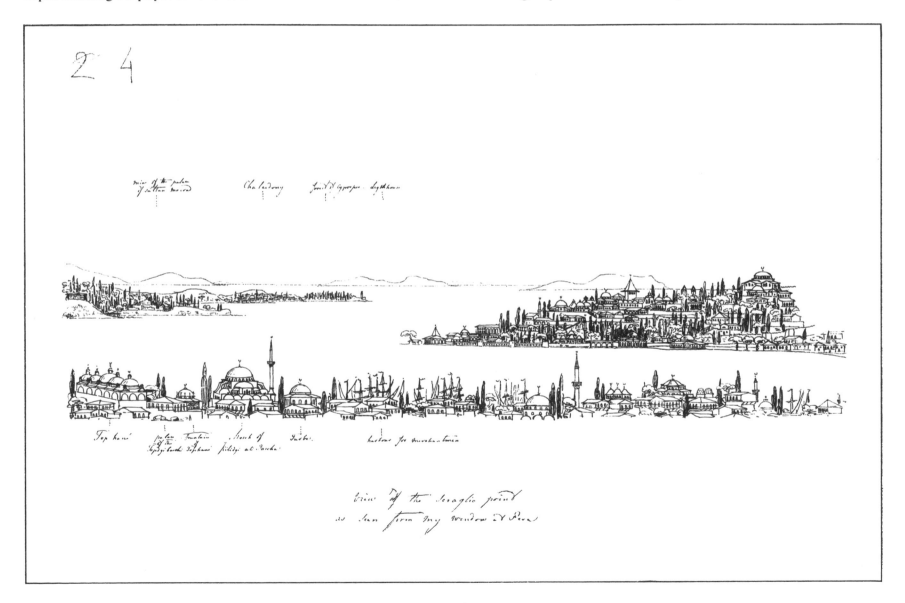

of Modern Costume. His scientific interest in the subject assisted by his skilled handling of the pen allowed him to create impeccable records of traditional Greek costume. His compositions of people in local costume reveal his delight in observation but, nevertheless, the figures are not treated merely as costume studies. They always have life and variety and are shown as conversing in natural groups. The people are usually depicted as going about their everyday business, as for example in pls 9-10, or being unconventionally placed in their local scenery. This testifies not only to Hope's concern with the successful staging of his figures, but also to his ability in capturing - with an economy of means - the typical features of each particular locality. Note, for example, the setting he has constructed for the *Women of Myconos* in pl.6. In the same way, his rapid handling of interiors is equally vivid, as for example in pls 1, 11, where his facility of composition gives freshness to the scene. His inventive drawing of the intimate scene in pl.7 is executed with manifest enjoyment. Figures wearing the same type of costume are usually rendered in various poses so that one might clearly perceive the way in which the different articles of each costume can be worn. Often the figures are drawn as performing various gestures, a device which not only adds to the liveliness of the scene but which also allows the artist to emphasise certain interesting details from the different pieces of each costume. In the scene with the *Albanians and the Moreot* (pls 2-3) the acuteness of this perception extends to every embroidered motif as well as every decorative accessory of the costume. His drawings of head-dresses (pls 15-17) are like close-ups where each "portrait" is a charming specimen of Hope's sensitive penwork and expressive of varying textures.

Hope possesses the skills of a miniaturist. In his panoramic views he is capable of drawing people whose size is not more than a few millimeters but who are nevertheless active and lively. In his long, low panoramic views, each site is meticulously treated down to the slightest detail, such as the mountain paths in the *View of Mount Athos* (pl.61), the tiniest Turkish pavilion on the quay of *Nafplion* (pl.56) or the Lilliputian bell-towers in the *View of Zante* (pl.95). In the panorama of *The town of Rhodes* (pls 92-93) where the suburbs of the city are shown to the right, every house and tree is depicted in admirable microscopic exactness. The same applies to the *View of Syros* (pl.81) where the town is drawn as in a minute linear puzzle. By means of the virtuosity of his outline, Hope brings to life the atmosphere of Greek towns without any unnecessary embellishments as, for example, in the *View of Athens* (pl.24). The views of the islands are rendered with the utmost delicacy, while his draughtsmanship is combined with a fine sense of composition. In the views of *Aegina* (pl.66), *Hydra* (pl.68), *Tinos* (pl.76) and *Myconos* (pl.74), the perspective of numerous architectural elements is correctly drawn and manifests the degree to which he could master complex detail. In his *View of Naxos* as seen through the gigantic archaic gate (pl.90) he has succeeded in giving a successful impression of size and spaciousness. A variety of architectural details such as the *Tombs in Mycenae* (pls 49-53) and *The Lion Gate* (pl.48), or a number of ancient pieces of sculpture that he saw in the course of his tour, have been put down on paper by means of vigorous pen work, as in pls 28, 62-63, 89.

Being primarily a draughtsman, Hope employs a simple scheme of colour. The majority of the drawings are made with pen or ink and sepia wash. The views of *Paros* (pl.85), *Tinos* (pl.77), *Myconos* (pl.75) and *Hydra* (pl.70), although subdued in colour, are far from monotonous; dashed in with washes of sepia they convey the very spirit of sunshine, largely achieved by the untouched patches of the paper. Particularly successful is the light effect in the drawing of *The Dove-Cote* (pl.80) and of *The Fountain of Hassan Pascha* (pl.59) which also reveal Hope's brilliance in expressing - economically - form and tone. It is on a basis of pen drawing that Hope laid his colour in simple washes, such as in the *Monument of Salamis* (pl.100), or the temples of *Corinth* (pl.42) and *of Apollo Epicurius* (pl.101) where he has achieved an unpretentious clarity. In the watercolours as, for example, in the two views of *The Lysicrates Monument* (pls 98-99) and *The Theseion* (pl.97), he uses a limited palette of transparent colours such as blue-gray, yellow, brown and pale blue broadly laid over the pencil lines; the graceful colour effect is brightened by touches of red. In *Naxos* (pl.102) the whiteness of the ancient gate contrasts with the blue-gray of the background and produces a vivid impression of the texture of the marble sparkling under the clear sky.

From the drawings in the Benaki Museum it is clear that while he was foremost a recorder, at the same time Hope was not indifferent to the physical charm of the Greek scene. Besides the proficiency and precision that characterises Hope's Greek drawings, their luminosity and freshness testify to the artist's enjoyment at the aspect of the world before his eyes. Moreover, Hope's power of drawing subtly and suggestively makes our imagination multiply and extend the details. However, in addition to the aesthetic pleasure it affords the spectator, this collection has a further significance: it is through this treasure of material that Hope has handed down a vast and faithful record of his visit to Greece. There is no doubt that for a series of authentic pictures of Greek scenery, costume and architecture before 1800 we must look at the Hope collection.

"History must have its illustrators; and none of them are more useful than the actual illustrators of the time, the artists", Sir Steven Runciman points out[5]. The Hope collection of drawings constitutes a pictorial inventory of original information which makes an invaluable contribution to our knowledge of eighteenth century Greece.

NOTES

1. Gennadeios Library, Arch 1047.3.
2. D. Watkin, *Thomas Hope and the Neo-Classical Idea,* London, 1968, p. 5.
3. Inv. No 27251 which is a pen drawing (20 × 22cm) of an ancient bronze sculpture, is inscribed in Hope's writing "drawn by Mr Fauvel" (pl.64). Inv. No 27252 is a pencil drawing (20 × 22cm) of an ancient relief and is signed "Fauvel" (pl. 65).
4. *Observations on the Plans and Elevations designed by James Wyatt Architect for Downing College Cambridge, in a letter to Francis Annesley Esq. M.P., by Thomas Hope,* London, 1804.
5. F. M. Tsigakou, *The Rediscovery of Greece,* London 1981, Introduction.

CATALOGUE OF THE ILLUSTRATIONS

Athenian Women

Moriote Greek

Albanians

Athenian Woman   Greek of the Morea   & Details of the Albanian Costume

Hydriotes.

Greeks of Micony

Women of Micony

Women of Naxos

Women of Chio   Papas

Tchaoosch of the Captan Pasha. Caleondgi Tacorhan. Women of Mitylene.

Tchawoush bashi Smirniote hamals

Smirniote Greeks

Woman of Smirna

Fanariotes.

Woman of Chio.

Greek or Tacoshan dancing Boys.

Embass.r Janisary. Caleondgi Greek dancing boys.

Tartar Messenger Greek lady French Merch'ts Wife Embass'r Janisary Greek lady   Greek Woman Facoshaw.

Chiote   Lesbian   Chiote   Chiote   Chiote

Chiote   Smyrniote   Perote   Smyrniote

Chiote   Fanariote   Greek Sailor   Woman of Athens   Lesbian

Capitan Pasha's Tchawoosh   Greek lady   Taooshan   Greek papas   Topdgi

Turkish child   Turk Wrapped in his Shawl   Asiatic   Calendgi   Taooshan

16

Combaradgi   Tattar Messenger   Common Turban   Greek Lady   Calioidgi

Effendi   Tergiuman   Reis   Jenissary in Gala dress

Visir   Common Turban   Embassador Jenissary   Bash Tchaworish   Trooshan

17

73

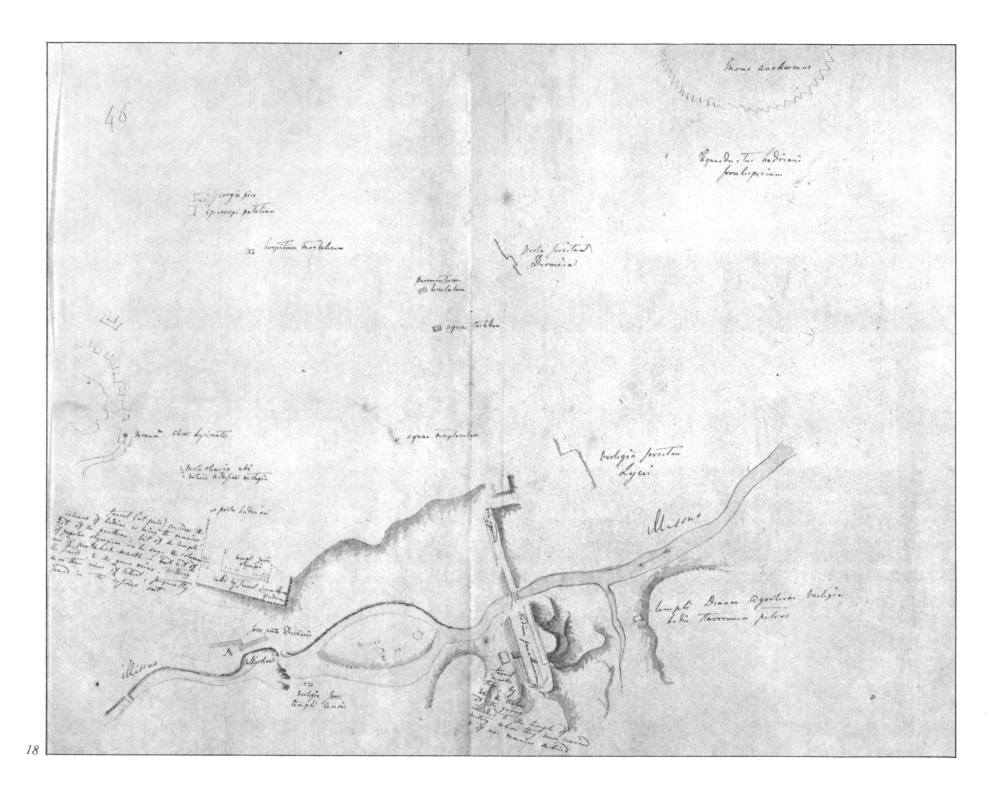

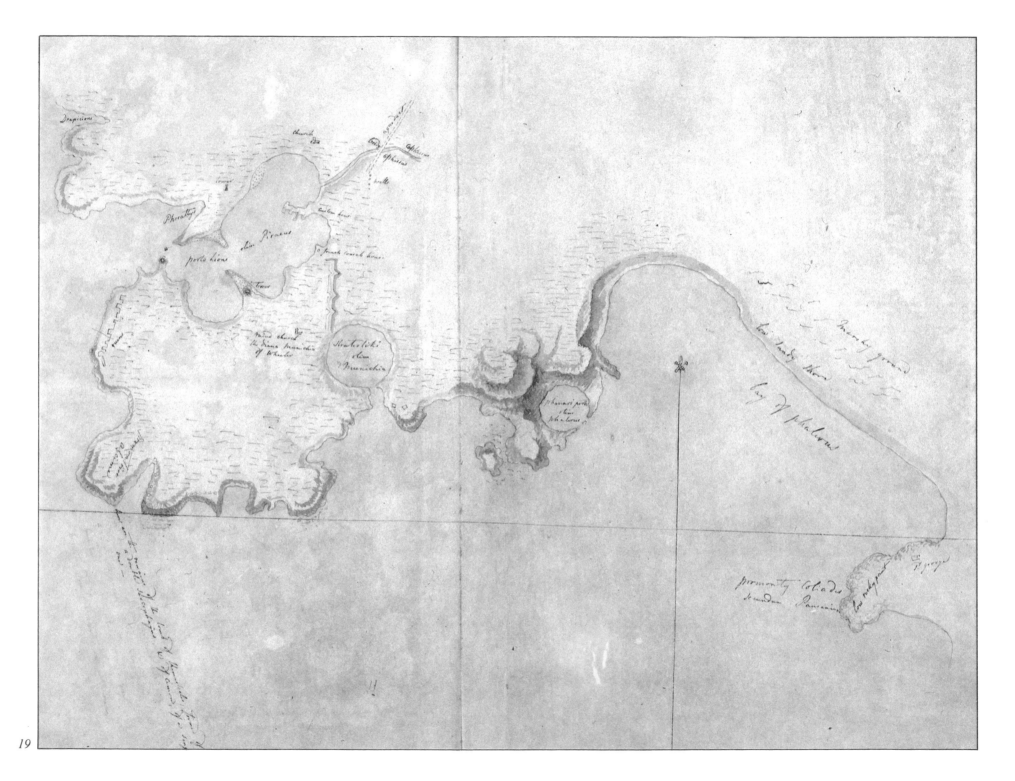

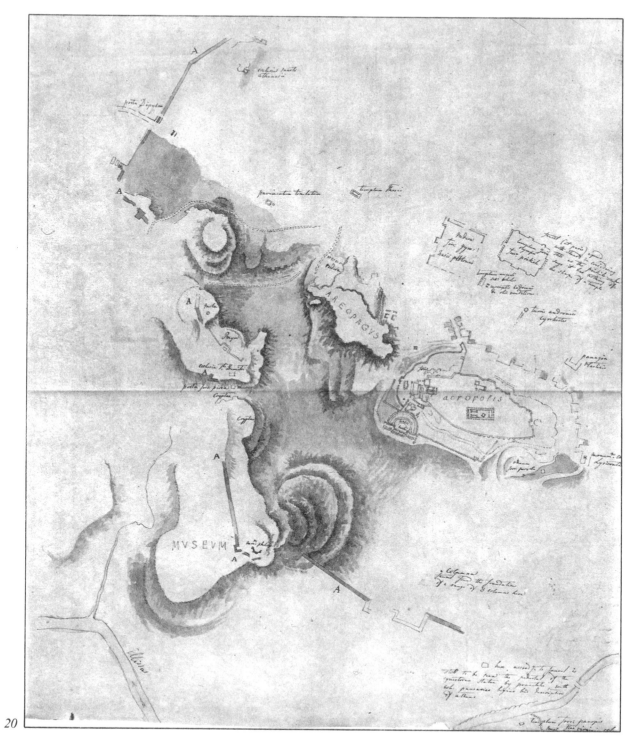

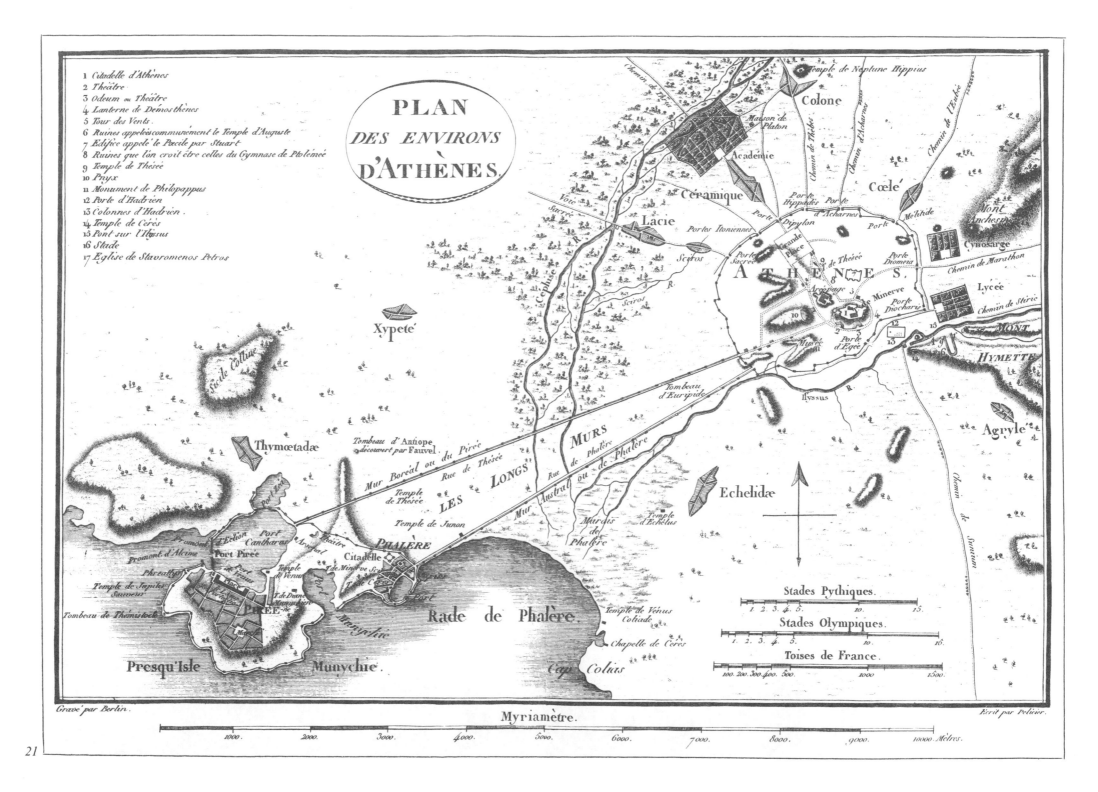

PLAN
DES ENVIRONS
D'ATHÈNES.

1 Citadelle d'Athènes
2 Théâtre
3 Odeum ou Théâtre
4 Lanterne de Démosthènes
5 Tour des Vents.
6 Ruines appelées communément le Temple d'Auguste
7 Edifice appelé le Pœcile par Stuart
8 Ruines que l'on croit être celles du Gymnase de Ptolémée
9 Temple de Thésée
10 Pnyx
11 Monument de Philopappus
12 Porte d'Hadrien
13 Colonnes d'Hadrien.
14 Temple de Cérès
15 Pont sur l'Ilyssus
16 Stade
17 Eglise de Stavromenos Petros

Temple de Neptune Hippius
Colone
Maison de Platon
Académie
Chemin de Thria
Chemin de Thebes
Chemin d'Acharnes
Chemin de l'Eubée
Cœlé
Mont Anchesme
Céramique
Voie Sacrée
Port Hippades Port d'Acharnes
Porte Dipylon
Melithide
Lacie
Portes Itoniennes
Cephise R.
Porte Sacrée
Grande Place
Porte de Thésée
Porte Diomea
Porte
Cynosarge
Sciros
ATHÈNES.
Xypeté
Sciros R.
Argopage
10
T. de Minerve
Lycée
Chemin de Marathon
Porte Diocharis
12
13
Chemin de Stirie
Su le Colias
Musée
Porte d'Egée
MONT
HYMETTE
Tombeau d'Euripide
Ilyssus R.
Agryle
Thymœtadæ
Tombeau d'Antiope découvert par Fauvel
Mur Boréal ou du Pirée
Rue de Thésée
LES LONGS MURS
Rue de Phalère
Rue de Phalère
Echelidæ
Temple de Thésée
Mur Austral ou de Phalère
Temple de Junon
Marais de Phalère
Temple d'Echelus
Promont. d'Alcime
L'Eétion Port Cantharus
Port Pirée
Arsenal
Théâtre
Citadelle
PHALÈRE
Phreattys
Temple de Venus
T. de Minerve Scir.
T. de Cérès
Stades Pythiques.
Temple de Jupiter Sauveur
T. de Diane Munychien
Port
1. 2. 3. 4. 5.
10.
15.
Tombeau de Thémistocle
PIRÉE
Munychie
Rade de Phalère.
Temple de Vénus Coliade
Stades Olympiques.
1. 2. 3. 4. 5.
10.
16.
Presqu'Isle
Munychie.
Cap Colias
Chapelle de Cérès
Toises de France.
100. 200. 300. 400. 500.
1000.
1500.

Gravé par Berlin.

Écrit par Pelicier.

Myriamètre.

1000.   2000.   3000.   4000.   5000.   6000.   7000.   8000.   9000.   10000. Mètres.

21

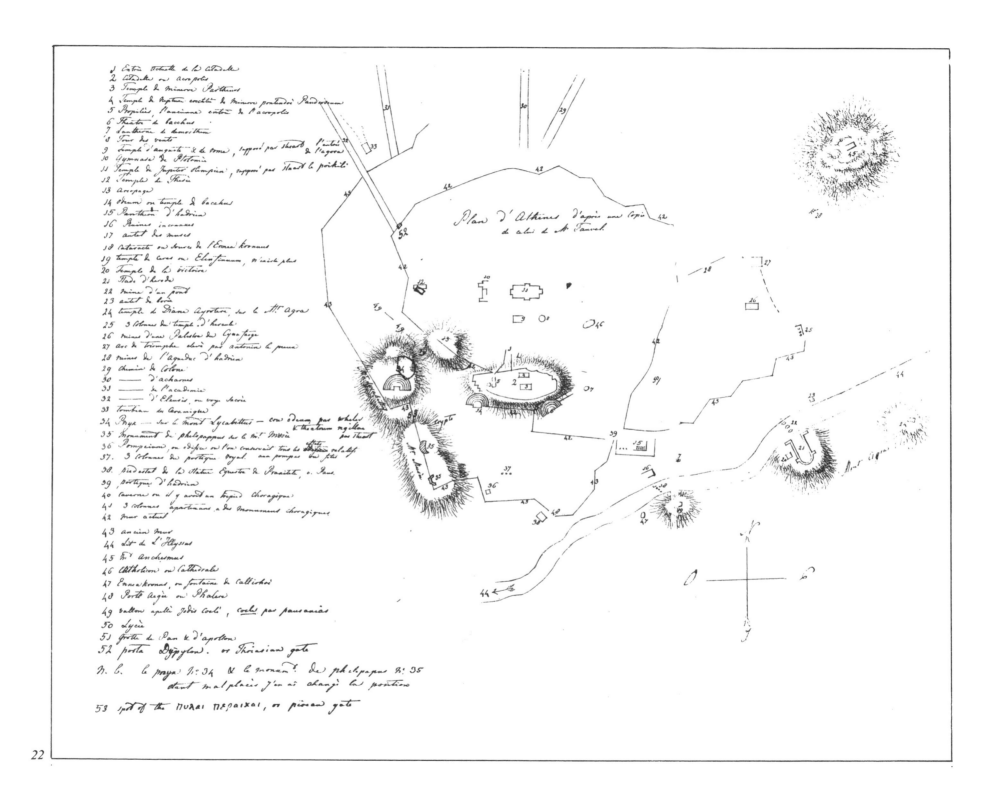

Plan d'Athènes d'après une copie de celui de M. Fauvel.

1 Entrée actuelle de la Citadelle
2 Citadelle ou acropolis
3 Temple de Minerve Parthénon
4 Temple de Neptune erechtée de Minerve pontia dei Pandrosum
5 Propylées, l'ancienne entrée de l'acropolis
6 Théatre de Bacchus
7 lanthénion de Demosthène
8 Tour des vents
9 Temple d'auguste & de Rome, supposé par Stuart l'entrée de l'agora
10 Gymnase de Ptolémie
11 Temple de Jupiter Olympien, supposé par Stuart le poïkile
12 Temple de Thesée
13 Aréopage
14 Odeum ou temple de Bacchus
15 Panthéon d'hadrien
16 Ruines inconnues
17 autel des muses
18 cataracte ou source de l'Ennea Kronous
19 temple de Cerès ou Eleusinum, n'existe plus
20 Temple de la victoire
21 Stade d'Herode
22 ruine d'un pont
23 autel de borée
24 temple de Diane Agrotère, sur le Mt. Agra
25 3 colonnes du temple d'hercule
26 ruines d'une Palestre du Gymnase
27 Arc de Triomphe elevé par antonin le pieux
28 ruines de l'aqueduc d'hadrien
29 chemin de Coloné
30 ——— d'acharnes
31 ——— de l'academie
32 ——— d'Eleusis, ou voye sacrée
33 Tombeau du Ceramique
34 Pnyx — sur le mont Lycabettus — con odeum par Wheler & theatrum agillea par Stuart
35 Monument de philopappus sur le Mt. Musée
36 Pompeium, ou edifice ou l'on conservait tous les choses relatif
37 3 colonnes du portique royal aux pompes ou fêtes
38 Piedestal de la Statue Equestre de Praxitèle, ou Paus.
39 portique d'hadrien
40 caverne ou il y avait un trepied Choragique
41 3 colonnes apartenans à des monuments choragiques
42 mur actuel
43 ancien mur
44 Lit de l'Ilyssus
45 Mt. Anchesmus
46 Catholicon ou Cathédrale
47 Ennea Kronous, ou fontaine de Callichoï
48 Porte Aegée ou Phalere
49 vallon apellé Jedis Coeli, coeli par pausanias
50 Lycée
51 Grotte de Pan & d'apollon
52 porta Dijpylon. or Thriasian gate

N. B. le pnyx N. 34 & le monument de philopappus N. 35
étant malplacés j'en ai changé la position

53 spot of the ΠΥΛΑΙ ΠΕΡΑΙΚΑΙ, or piroean gate

22

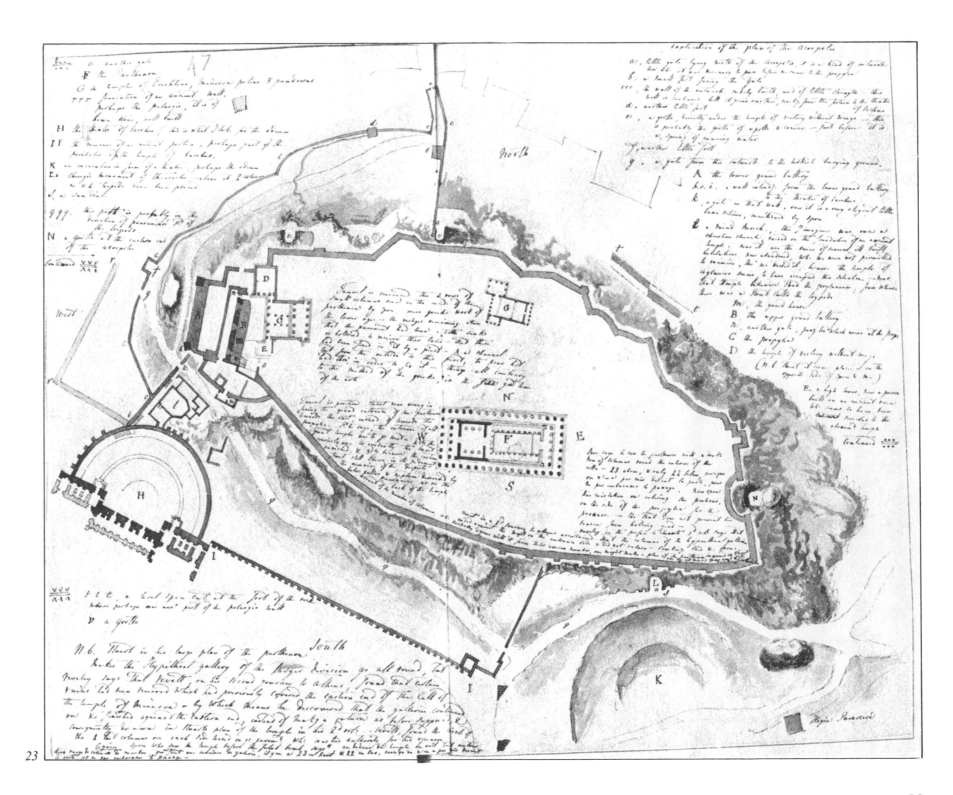

23

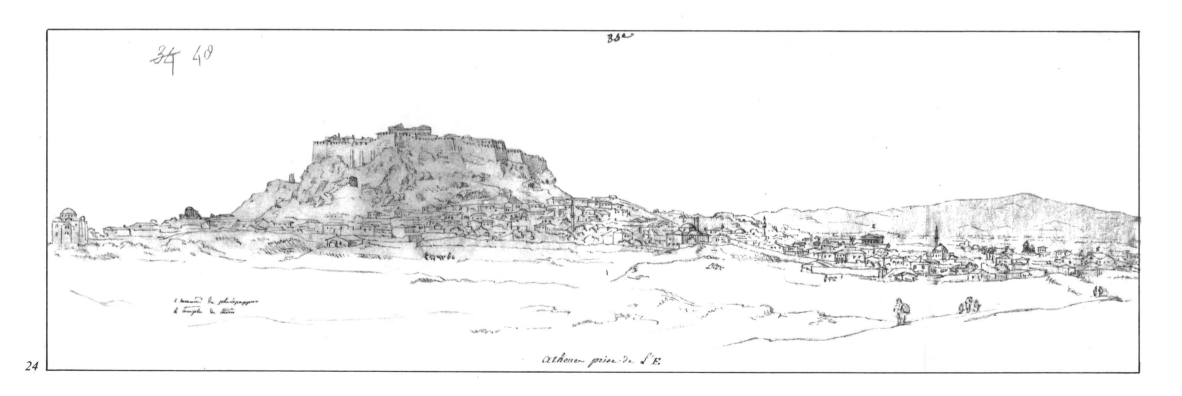

à demander les photographies
& temple de Thésée

Carobi

Athènes prise de l'E.

24

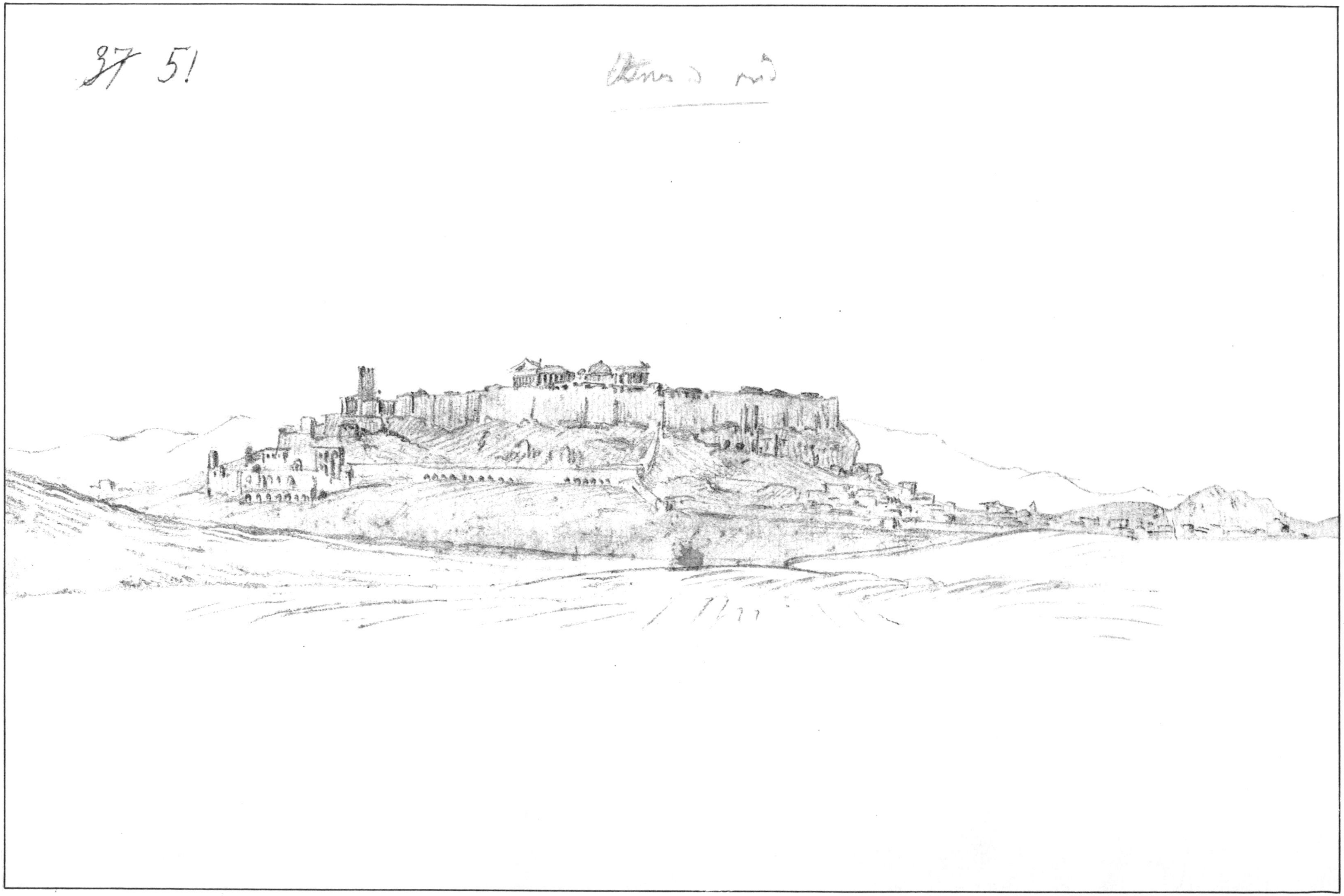

25

Citadelle d'athenes

Bas Reliefs du Temple de minerve.

Basrelief of the parthenon, Athens

Basrelief in Sig.r Logotheti's Certile at Athens

28

Basrelief in the Acropolis at Athens & group of Calenders

103

Vue des propilées prise de l'O

4E 56

Vue du Théâtre d'Athènes prise du S.O. E

31

32

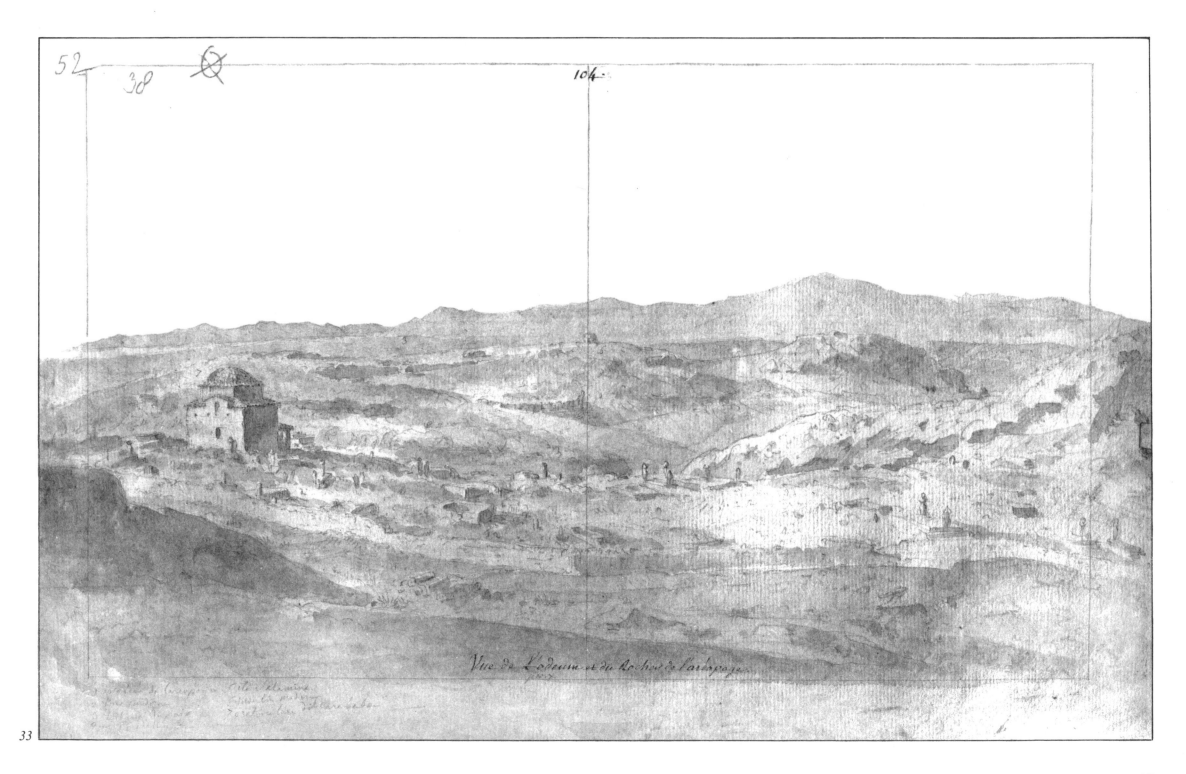

52

38

104.

Vue de l'Odeum et du Rocher de l'aréopage.
1817

33

105

Capuchin Convent & Lanthern of Demosthenes at Athens.

34

107

35

109

84ᵉ

35
49

Tombeau taillé dans le Roc Sur le Chemin d'athènes a phalere

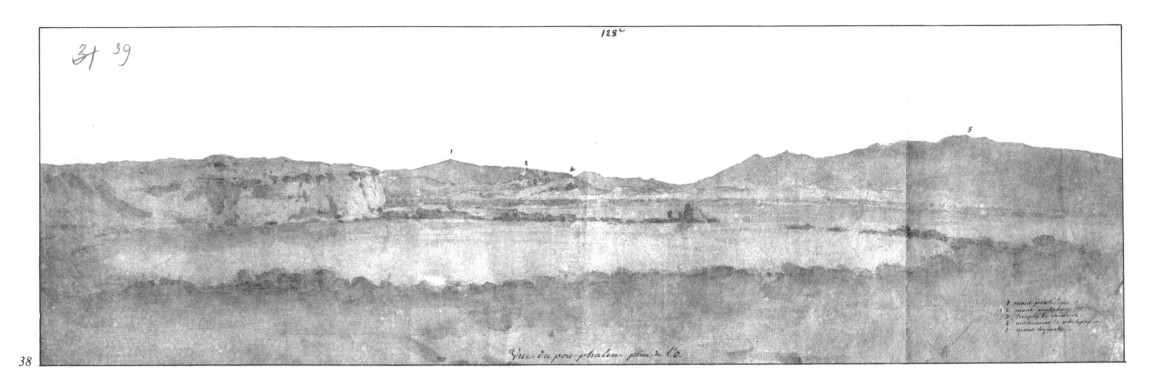

128°

3f 39

5

1 mont pentelique
2 mont anchesmes
3 temple de minerve
4 monument de philopappus
5 mont hymette

38

Vue du port phalere prise de l'O.

80°

4f 60

4

7

2

3

6

1 porte de caret
2 isle salamine
3 les débris de deux
4 église sur les ruines d'un temple
5 caserne
6 ruines ionique
7 aqueduc

39

Lepsine (Eleusis) prise du S.E.

28 36

40

Vue du Cap Colonne prise du N

A isle St george d'arba

Vue du temple de Minerve Suniade
au Cap Colonne.

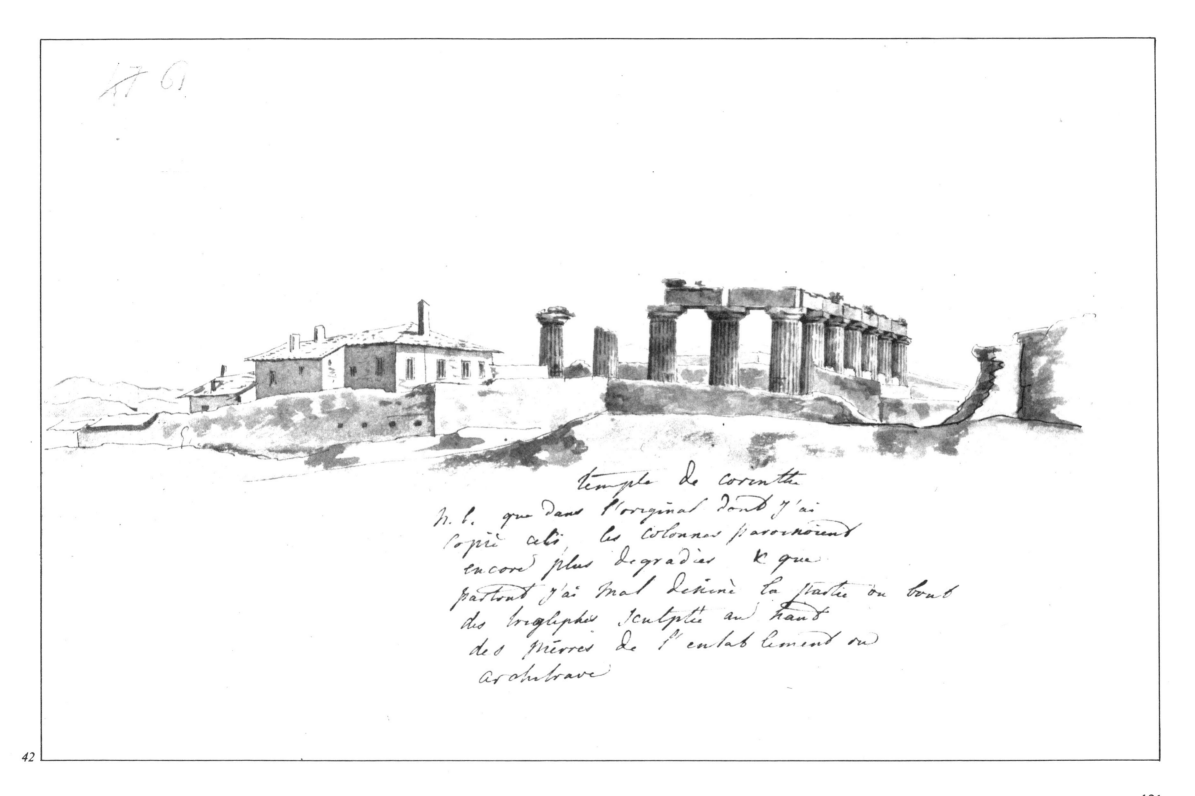

Temple de Corinthe
n.b. que dans l'original dont j'ai
copié celi, les colonnes paroissoient
encore plus degradées & que
partout j'ai mal dessiné la partie ou bout
des triglyphes sculptée au haut
des pierres de l'entablement ou
architrave

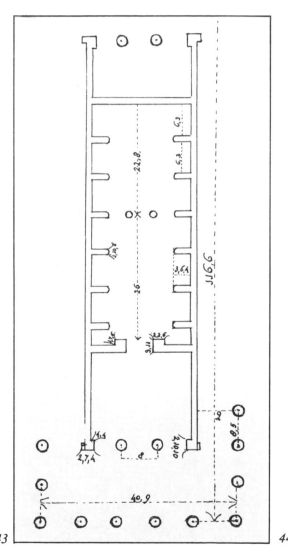

43

Temple de Nemée. Ce temple
est à 5 lieus de Corinthe
N.B. que la longueur des proportionée
des colomnes n'ont pas une faute
du dessin mais existé reellement

la fontaine adrastée est à
500 toises de ce monument
sur le chemin de Corinthe
à Yanari

44

123

_ platform or uplands of the citadel
_ _ gate of the Lions
_ _ _ wall of the Cyclops
_ wall of Agamemnons Tomb

Mycenae

_ bed of the torrent at the bottom of the
precipice whi: separates the uplands of the
citadel from the mountain behind it

45

Mycene.

46

Gate of the Lions Mycenae

47

Gate of the Cyclops at Mycenae

N.b. The top stone with the lions measures 10½ ft in height, & the under

part uncovered, wh: serves to light the chamber

Treasury of Atreus, Mycenae

49

133

50

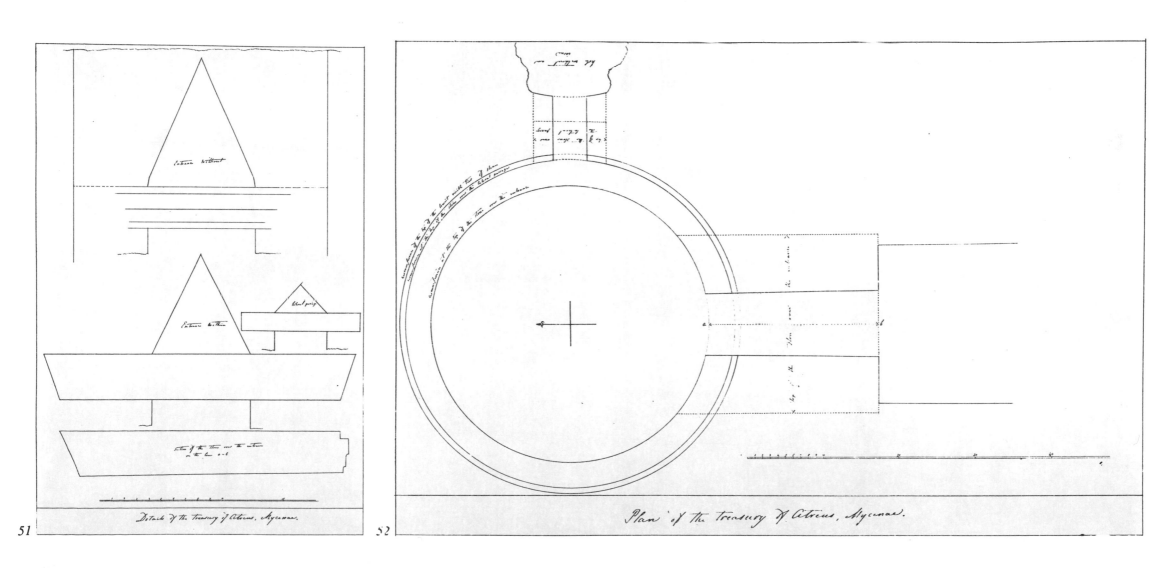

Details of the Treasury of Atreus, Mycenae.

Plan of the Treasury of Atreus, Mycenae.

51

52

137

Entrance of the Treasury of Atreus, Mycenae

53

Naples de Romanie prise de l'O.

Nauplia   Palamidi

56

Nauplia   *Palamidi*

57

145

fountain of Hanan Pacha
at hauplia

Fountain of Hassan Pascha at Nauplia.

40

60

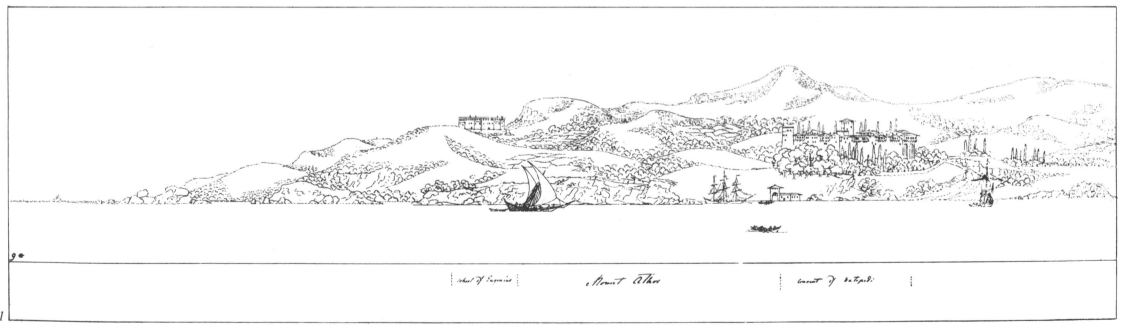

9*

school of Eugenius   Mount Athos   convent of Batopedi

61

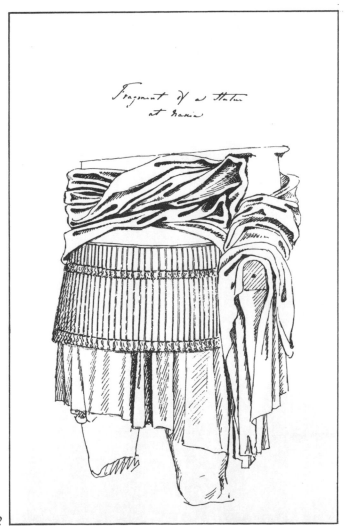

Fragment of a Statue
at Rome

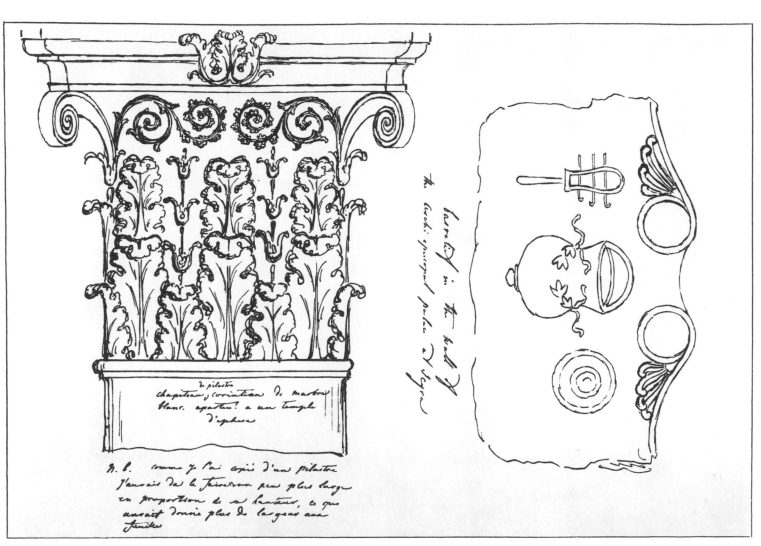

de pilastre
chapiteau, corinthien de marbre
blanc, apartient a un temple
d'éphese

N. B.   comme je l'ai copié d'un pilastre
j'aurais fait le frivoleron peu plus large
en proportion de sa hauteur, ce qui
aurait donné plus de largeur aux
feuilles

62

63

153

64

Figure of bronze a vase of clay found at Troy of a known supposed to be that of Achilles by Mr Michael ....

Drawn by ....

ff 67

Copy from the original drawing in the possession of Mr Walters

65

ff 67

ΑΔΑΜΑΣ
ΟΔΡΥΣΗΣ
ΝΥΜΦΑΙΣ

a Vase drawing in Carricar

Vue de la Ville d'Egine - isle d'Egine prise du N.O.

Vue du Temple de jupiter panellensien dans l'isle d'Egine prise du S.E.

Town & Harbour of Hydra.

Town of Hydra seen from my Reis house

Town & Harbour of Hydra

Town of Hydra seen from the platform of my reïs's house

66

58

hydra prise de l'entrée E du port.

72

Delos

73

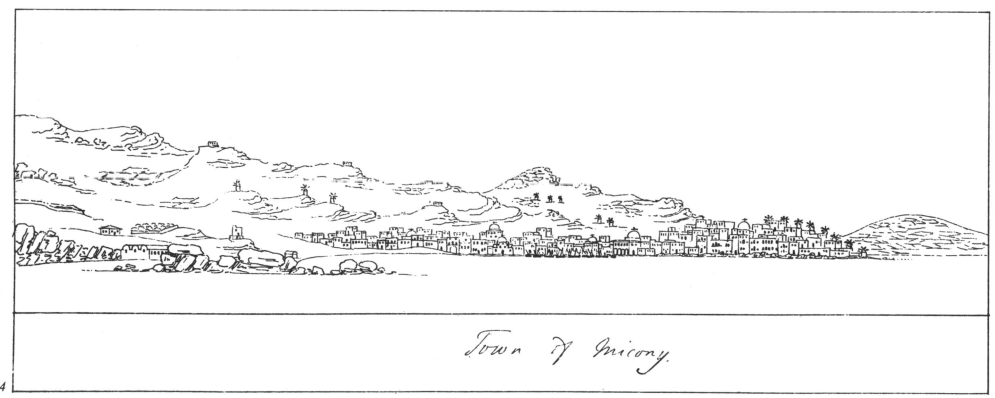

Town of Micony.

74

169

Town of Micony.

38

Island & town of Tinos

76

173

Island & Town of Tinos

77 37

175

78

177

Mill at Paros with 8 wings
& little sail between each wing.

79

Mill at Paros with eight wings
and intermediate sails.

80

179

Town of Scyra

Town of Scyra.

Grotto of Antiparos

83

View of the Town
of Paros

84

Town of Paros

85 36

189

Pigeon house of Tino
The lettice work made of bricks

86

Dovecot at Tino

87

a Santorin Château de Scaro vû de l'Est

colonne non achevé sur la Montagne d'apollon a
3 lieues de la ville le naxie
prise de la mer a un 1/2 de lieue du village de comiacki

55

89

68

Unfinished Door Way of a Temple at Paros.

90

195

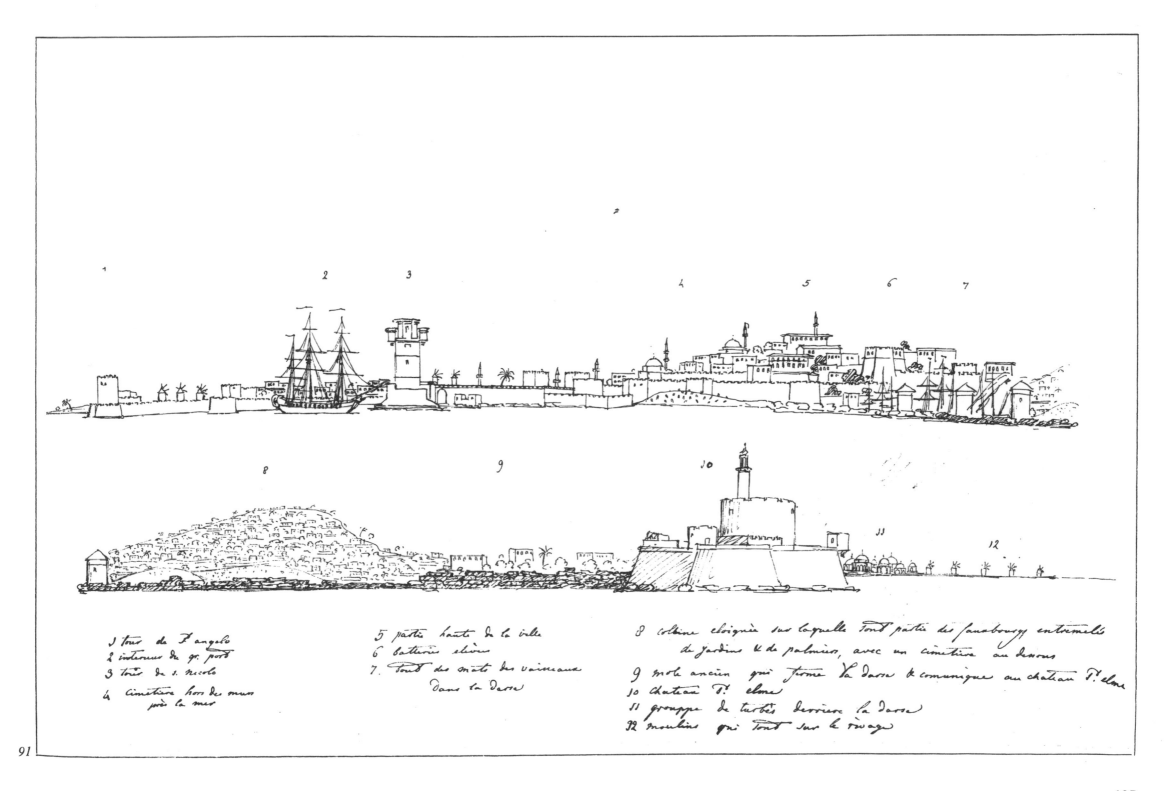

1 tour de S.t angelo
2 intérieur du gr. port
3 tour de s. nicolo
4 cimetière hors des murs
       près la mer

5 partie haute de la ville
6 batteries élevées
7 tout des mats des vaisseaux
       dans la darse

8 colline éloignée sur laquelle sont partie des fauxbourgs entremêlés
       de jardins & de palmiers, avec un cimetière au dessous
9 môle ancien qui ferme la darse & communique au château S.t elme
10 château S.t elme
11 groupe de turbés derrière la darse
12 moulins qui sont sur le rivage

91

92

93

199

𝒹 109

Vue de la montagne palæo Castro d'anon L'isle de Thiaki
suir laquelle on prétend qu'étoit le palais d'Ulisse

94

95   Suite de la Vue du port de Zante prise au milieu du port.

96   Vue de Corfou du Coté de l'Est prise en mer.

98

99

temple dorique dans la Morée
sur une montagne près du fleuve alphée
& de Caritena

65

n.b. que ce
morceau représentant
une partie de la corniche avec les métopes
est mal dessiné & devrait
être ainsi

n.b. qu'on
aperçoit telle échancrure
en haut des canelures des triglyphes qui
se voyent dans la façade restaurée

Door way of the unfinished Temple on the rocks at Paros

103

ANNOTATED CATALOGUE OF THE PLATES

The drawings in each volume are numbered in succesive numerical order for volumes I - III (numbers 1-99) and in a new numerical order for volumes IV and V independently (numbers 1 - 109 and 1 -61 respectively). The numeration is probably arranged by Hope himself; many numbers have been erased and corrected, while on certain drawings two different numbers are indicated, one in pencil and another in ink.

Our classification (i.e. Inv. No) has given each drawing - throughout the 5 volumes - its own successive number.

vol. I,   Inv. No 27052-27102   Pages: 33. Greek Subjects: 0
vol. II,   Inv. No 27103-27141   Pages: 31. Greek Subjects: 20, Inv. Nos 27110-27141
vol. III, Inv. No 27142-27183   Pages: 33. Greek Subjects: 15, Inv. Nos 27142-27156
vol. IV,   Inv. No 27184-27297   Pages: 108. Greek Subjects: 44, Inv. Nos 27211-27297
vol. V   Inv. No 27298-27380   Pages: 62. Greek Subjects: 17, Inv. Nos 27307-27375

The measurements of the pages are, in volumes I - IV 36 × 49.5cm, and in volume V 39 × 60cm. It was however thought necessary to indicate separately the measurements of each drawing, because there is often more than one drawing on the same page, whilst on other occasions the drawings have been executed on sheets of paper which have afterwards been pasted on the pages of the volumes.

The plates are catalogued from 1-103 for the purpose of this publication; the numeration is unconnected either with Hope's numbers or the Benaki's inventory.

1. Athenian Women - A Moreot

Sepia drawing on paper 36 × 49.5cm. Inv. *No* 27141. Inscribed:
"66 - Athenian Women - Moreote Greek".
Here is an incident in the daily life of an Athenian household: mother and daughter are seated on the sofa and the maid serves them with refreshments. They watch two women dance. This dance, only performed by women and featuring slow movements of the out-stretched arms, is the one referred to by travellers as the "Up - Down" dance. (cf. O. M. Baron von Stackelberg, *Trachten und Gebräuche der Neugriechen*, Berlin, 1831, plate 3).

2. Men and Women of Albania

Sepia drawing on paper 36 × 49.5cm. Inv. *No* 27155. Inscribed:
"Albanians".

Foreign travellers used the name "Albanians" to describe the people whom the Greeks call "Arvanites", people of Albanian origin living in Greece. The Arvanites in this drawing had settled on the edge of Attica and their costume is that which is now referred to as the "Mesoghitiki" (see M. Michael-Dede, *The Costume of Messoghitissa*, Athens, 1981, in Greek).

3. Details of the Albanian costume - An Athenian Woman - A Moreot

Sepia drawing on paper 36 × 49.5cm. Inv. *No* 27156. Inscribed:
"Athenian woman - Greek of the Morea and details of the albanian costume".
The Athenian woman is depicted at the top left and the Moreot to the right. Below are details of the "Segouni" worn by the Albanian woman in the drawing Cat. No 2. The jewellery in the centre is the so-called Kambos, which was used to hold the braid of hair (cf. pl. No 2). The Albanian's stockings are called "Touzloukia". The hair style is interesting: only the top of the head is shaven and the rest of the hair falls freely, whereas the heads of the Epirot Albanians are entirely shaven except for one lock at the top.

4. Men and Women of Hydra

Sepia drawing on paper 36 × 49.5cm. Inv. *No* 27153. Inscribed:
"Hydriotes".
Here Hope employs his usual device of representing the inhabitants in various poses so that their costume may be seen from all sides. For the costume of Hydra see: F. M. Tsigakou, *The Greek Costume, Printed Sources, 15th-19th century*, (in Greek), Exhibition Catalogue, Athens, 1980, p. 59.

5. Men and Women of Myconos

Sepia drawing on paper 36 × 49.5cm. Inv. *No.* 27138. Inscribed:
"63 - Greeks of Micony".
In this drawing Hope skilfully portrays costumes from several of the island's social types.

6. Women of Mykonos

Sepia drawing on paper 36 × 49.5cm. Inv. *No* 27137 Inscribed:
"62 - Women of Micony".
The rendering of the three women in various poses shows how the different articles of

the costume can be worn. It is interesting to note the economy with which Hope has constructed a setting where typical architectural characteristics of the island appear (e.g. the church and the windmill).

7. Men and Women of Naxos

Sepia drawing on paper 36 × 49.5cm. Inv. *No* 27139. Inscribed:
"64 - Women of Naxos".
The group of four figures to the left creates an intimate and humorous scene. The observer is amused by the combination of the Naxiot woman who is spinning with the help of a male relative and the 'Frankish - looking' lady who is being offered the traditional refreshments.

8. Chiot women and a Greek priest

Sepia drawing on paper 36 × 49.5cm. - Inv. *No* 27130. Inscribed:
"57 - Women of Chio - Papas".
For the costume of Chiot women as well as the costumes of priests, see: F. M. Tsigakou, op. cit (Cat No 4), p. 58, 59.
The women of Chios were often depicted by foreign travellers, because they had the reputation of being the most elegant as well as the most friendly women in Greece. cf. F. Atgentis, *Chios by Geographers and Travellers from the 8th to the 20th C.*, 2 vols, Athens, 1946, (in Greek).

9. Greek and Turkish costumes

Sepia drawing on paper 36 × 49.5cm. Inv. *No* 27126. Inscribed:
"53 - Tchawoosh of the Capitan Pasha - Caleondgi - Taooshan - Women of Mitylene".
The first two Turkish titles are, in order: "Admiral's Page" - "Sailor".
For "Taooshan", see Cat. No 17. For the costume of Mytilene during the period before the Greek Revolution, see: F. M. Tsigakou, op. cit. (cat. No 4), p. 58.

10. Greek and Turkish costumes

Sepia drawing on paper 36 × 49.5cm. - Inv. *No* 27127. Inscribed:
"54 - Tchawoosh bashi - Smirniote hamals - Smirniote Greeks - Woman of Smirna".
The title "Tchawoosh bashi" is a variation of "Bash Tchawoosh", that is "Chief - Attendant" (cf. Cat. No 17). For the costume of the Greeks of Smyrna, see F. M. Tsigakou, op. cit. (Cat. No 34), p. 59.

11. Scene in the interior of a Phanariot house

Sepia drawing on paper 36 × 49cm. Inv. No 27114. Inscribed:
"45 - Fanariotes - woman of Chio".
In this scene, the girl who is serving is a Chiot. The ladies of the house have the same hair-style as in pl. Nos 16-17. The costume of the Phanariot was similar to that worn by Greek archontes, that is a fur coat and a top hat, cf. F. M. Tsigakou, op. cit. (cat. No 4), p. 57.

12. "May - pole"

Sepia drawing on paper 36 × 49.5cm. Inv. *No* 27117. Inscribed:
"48 - Greek or Taooshan dancing boys".
(cf. Cat. Nos 13, 17).

13. Greek and Turkish costumes

Sepia drawing on paper 36 × 49.5cm. Inv. *No* 27116. Inscribed:
"47 - Embassador's Jenissary - Caleondgi -Greek dancing boys".
This *Jenissary* and the *Caleondgi* are depicted in the drawing cat. No 17. The *Greek dancing boys* are the ones referred to as "Taooshan" (cf. cat. No 12 and cat. No 17).

14. Greek and Turkish Costumes

Sepia drawing on paper 36 × 49cm. Inv. *No* 27112. Inscribed:
"43 - Tartar messenger - Greek lady - French merchant's wife - Embassador's Jenissary - Greek lady - Greek woman - Taooshan".
It is interesting to note the distinction made here between the *Greek lady* and the *Greek woman*. The latter might belong to a lower class; however, her costume is richer in embroidery than that of the *Greek lady*.

15. Greek Head-dresses

Sepia drawing on paper 36 × 49.5cm. Inv. *No* 27130. Inscribed:
"58 - Chiote - Lesbian - Chiote - Chiote - Chiote - Chiote - Smyrniote - Perote - Smyrniote - Chiote - Fanariote - Greek Sailor - Woman of Athens - Lesbian".
The type of head-gear revealed one's profession, as for example in cat. No 17, as well as one's age, especially for women. Shown here are three variations of the head-dress of Chios, one of which is that of an elderly woman. Two variations of the head-dress of

Lesbos are also depicted. For the costume of the Perot woman, see: F. M. Tsigakou, op. cit. (cat. No 4), p. 32. For Greek head-dresses in general, see: K. G. Koré, *Greek head-dress*, Athens, 1978 (in Greek).

16. Turkish and Greek Head-dresses

Sepia drawing on paper 36 × 49cm. Inv. *No*. 27113 Inscribed:
"44 - Capitan Pasha's Tchawoosh - Greek lady - Taooshan - Greek Papas - Topdgi - Turkish child - Turk wrapped in his shawl - Asiatic - Caleondgi - Taooshan".
Tchawoosh means attendant (see cat. No 17); *Capitan Pasha* was the title given to the admiral - *Topdgi* means a gunner or artillery man - For the *Taooshan* and the *Caleondgi* see cat. No 17 - The *Greek woman* depicted here is a Phanariot (cf. pl. *No.*11).

17. Greek and Turkish Head-dresses

Pen and sepia drawing on paper 36 × 49cm. Inv. *No*. 27110. Inscribed:
"41 - Combaradgi - Tartar messenger - common turban - greek lady - Caleondgi - Effendi - Tergiuman - reis - Jenissary in Gala dress - visir - common turban - Embassador's Jenissary - Bash Tshawoosh - Taooshan".
Here are depicted various Turkish head-dresses, both military and civilian, and also that of a Greek woman. Head-gear has always revealed social status, rank, profession etc.
Combaradgi was a bombardier, or sailor on a fire - ship. *Caleondgi* was a sailor. *Tergiuman* was an interpreter. *Reis* means captain. *Visir* was one kind of prime minister. The *Tshawoush* were a special corps of 600 men who escorted the sultan to official ceremonies; the title *Bash Tshawoush* may be rendered as "Chief - Attendant" (Bash meaning leader). *Taooshan* or *Taooshin* literally means "bunnies", a name applied to boy-singers and dancers who entertained the court of the Sultan. *Tartar* was a courier. The Ottoman government employed a special corps of 200 couriers to despatch the correspondence of the state (see also pl.14). (The information above is extracted from the publication: M. D' Ohsson, *Tableau general de l' Empire Othoman*, 3 vols, Paris, 1820). The "Greek lady" must be from a Phanariot family of Constantinople because she is so indicated in the drawing Inv. *No* 27114 (cf. pl.11).

18. Map of Athens

Pen and watercolour drawing on paper 38 × 48cm. Inv. *No* 27229 Inscribed:
"46 - Mons Anchesmus - Giorgio Pio - Episcopi palatium - hospitium mentelicum -

porta forsitan Diomeia - aquae castullum - porta forsitan Diomeia - aquae castullum - vestigia Lycii - Monum. chor. Lysicrates - porta hadriani - Fauvel (at parts) considers the columns of hadrian as being the remains not of the pantheon, but of the temple of Jupiter Olympius, he says the columns are of pentelic marble - but not of the finest and the green veins, nothing more than veins of schist, frequently found in the inferior sort - temple Jovis olympius called by Fauvel pantéon d' Adrian - ilissus - fors porta Diocharis - callirhoe - vestigia fors templi cereris - via agresta - stadium panellenaicum - Fauvel marks steps, by which the victors of the games ascended to the temple of victory where they were crowned and of which remains subsist - templi Dianae agrotirae vestigiae hodie Stavromenos petros".

19. Map of the coastline from Piraeus to Phaleron

Pen and watercolour drawing on paper 47 × 37cm. Inv. *No* 27226. Inscribed:
"Drapicione - Phreattys - porto Lione olim Piraeus - promontoire alcione - here are the remains of the tomb of Themistocles formed of a double Sarcophagus and of Cimon, of a single one - Stratoniki - olim Munichia - phanari porto olim phalerus - bay of phalirus - promontory Coliades secundum Pausanium -bridge of Cephissus - custom house - french consul house - ruined church the Diana Munichia of Wheler - the sundy shore - marshy ground - St George"

20. Map of Athens

Pen and watercolour drawing on paper 46 × 37.5cm. Inv. *No*. 27228. Inscribed:
"45 - ecclesia sancta athanassi - A. porta Dipylon - tempium Thesei - rudera fors gymnasii Ptolemai - tempium Jovi Olympici fors poikili Fauvel (at parts) agreed with Stuart in considering this as the poikile - he says it has nothing of the shape of a temple - templum augustus segundum Wheler - inscriptio hadriani de oli vendition - turris andronici Cyrrhestes - Panagia Vlasticis - Monument cho. Lysicrates - Odeum forse Pericles - Colonna Fauvel found the foundation of a range of 3 columnns here - here, according to Fauvel is still to be seen the pedestal of the equestrian statue by Praxiteles with which pausanias begins his description of Athens-templum Jovis panopis nunc virginiis eccles. - A. mola A. Pnyx A. ecclesia St. Dimitrios A. porta forse pirae Cryptae".

21. Map of the environs of Athens

Engraving 23.5 × 33.5cm. Inv. *No* 27225.
Entitled: "Plan des environs d' Athènes". Undated. Inscribed: "Drawn by Pelicier,

Engraved by Berlin". The map originates from the book by Abbé Barthélemy, *Voyage du Jeune Anacharsis en Grèce*, Paris, 1788.

22. Map of Athens

Pen drawing on paper 33.5 × 43.5cm. Inv. *No* 27227. Inscribed:
"44 - plan of Athens d' après une copie dc celui de Mr Fauvel - 1. entrée actuelle de la citadelle - 2. citadelle ou Acropolis - 3. temple de Minerve Parthenos - 4. temple de Neptune erechtée de Minerve Pontendrose Pandroseum - 5. Propylées l' ancienne entrée de l' acropolis - 5. Theatre de bacchus - 7. Lanterne de Demosthène - 8. Tour de vents - 9. temple d' Auguste et de Rome, supposé par Stuart l' entrée de l' Agora - 10. Gymnase de Ptolemée - 11. Temple de Jupiter Olympien, supposé par Stuart le poikile - 12. Temple de Thesé - 13. Areopage - 14. Odeum ou temple de Bacchus - 15. Pantheon d' Adrien - 16. Ruines inconnues - 17. autel de Muses - 18. Cataracte ou Source de l' Enneakrounos - 19. temple de Ceres ou Elefsinium, n' existe plus - 20. temple de la Victoire - 21. Stade d' herode - 22. ruine d' un pont - 23. autel de boré - 24. temple de Diane Agrotera sur le Mt Agra - 25. 3 colonnes du temple d' hecube - 26. ruines d' une Palestre du Gynossarge - 27. arc de triomphe elevé par Antonin le pieux - 28. ruines de l' aqueduc d' hadrien - 29. chemin de colone - 30. d' acharnes - 31. de l' academie - 32. d' Eleusis ou voye sacré - 33. tombeau de ceramique - 34. Pnyx sur le mont Lycabettus - Odeum par Wheler et Theatrum Rigillae par Stuart - 35. Monument de Philopappus sur le mont Musée - 36. Pompeium ou édifice ou l' on conservait tous les objets relatifs aux pompes ou fetes - 37. 3 colonnes du portique royale - 38. piedestal de la statue Equeste de Praxitele, v. Paus. - 39. Portique d' Adrien - 40. caverne ou il avoit un trepied choragigue - 41. 3 colonnes appartenans a des monumentschoragiques - 42. mur actuel - 43. ancien mur - 44. Lit de l' Ilyssus - 45. Mt Anchesmus - 46. Catholicon ou Cathedrale - 47. Enneakrounos ou fontaine de Callirhoe - 48. Porte Aegée ou Phalere - 49. vallon appellé Jadis Coele, coeli par pausanias - 50. Lycée - 51. Grotte de Pan et d' Apollon - 52 Porta Dipylon or Thriasian Gate n.b. le pnyx no 34 et le monument de philopapus no 35 etant mal placés j' en ai changé la position - 53. spot of the ΠΥΛΑΙ ΠΕΡΑΙΧΑΙ or pirean gate".
(Map of Athens after a copy of that of Fauvel's - 1. the actual entrance of the citadel - 2. Citadel or Acropolis - 3. Temple of Minerva Parthenos - 4. temple of Neptune Erechteus of Minerva Pandroseian - 5. Propylaea the ancient entrance of the acropolis - 6. Theatre of bacchus - Lanterne of Demosthenes - 8. Tower of the Winds - 9. temple of Augustus and Rome, considered by Stuart the entrance of the Agora - 10. Gymnasium of Ptolemy - 11. Temple of Olympius Zeus considered by Stuart the poikile - 12.

Temple of Theseus - 13. Areopagus - 13. Odeum or temple of Bacchus - 15. Pantheon of Hadrian - 16. Unknown ruins - 17. altar of Muses - 18. Waterfall or Spring of Enneakrounos - 19. temple of Ceres or Elefsinium, it no longer exists - 20. temple of Victory - 21. Stadium of Herodes - 22. Ruins of a bridge - 23. Altar of Boreus - 24. temple of Diana Agrotera on Mt Agra - 25. 3 columns of the temple of Hecuba - 26. Ruins of a Palaestra of Cynossarges - 27. triumphal arch erected by Antoninus Pius - 28. ruins of Hadrian's Aqueduct - 29. road of Colonus - 30. of Acharnes - 31. of the Academy - 32. of Eleusis or sacred way - 33. tomb of Keramikos - 34. Pnyx on Mt Lycabcttus - Odeum by Wheler and Theatrum Rigillae by Stuart - 35. Monument of Philopappus - 36. Pompeium of edifice where all the objects relating to processions and festivals were guarded - 37. 3 columns of the royal portico - 38. pedestal of the equestrian statue of Praxiteles, v. Paus [anias] - 39. Hadrian's portico - 40. Cave where there was a choragic tripod - 41. columns belonging to choragic monuments - 42. present day wall - 43. ancient wall - 44. bed of Ilissus - 45. Mt Anchesmus - 46. Catholicon or Cathedral - 47. Enneakrounos or fountain of Kallirhoe - 48. Gate of Aegeus or Phaleron - 49. ravine called Coele, coeli by Pausanias - 50. Lyceum - 51. Grotto of Pan - 52. Dipylon Gate or Thriasian Gate n.b. the pnyx *No* 34 and the philopappus monument *No* 35 being wrongly placed I interchanged their position).

23. Plan of the Acropolis

Pen and watercolour drawing on paper 38.5 × 48.5cm. Inv. *No* 27230 Inscribed:
"explanation of the plan of the Acropolis - a little gate lying north of the Acropolis, it is a kind of outwork through which it was necessary to pass before one came to the propylaea - b. a small fort facing the gate - ccc the wall of the outwork rudily built and of little strength - this wall is continued till it joins another reaching from the fortress to the theatre of bachus - d. another little fort - e. a grotto; directly under the temple of victory without wings - this is probably the grotto of Apollo & Creusa - just before it is a spring of running water & another little fort g. a gate from this subwork to the turkish burrying ground.
A. the tower grand battery h.c.i. a wall extending to the tower grand battery h.c.i. a wall extending from the tower grand battery to the theatre of bacchus.
K. a gate in that wall over it is a very elegant little basso relievo, mentioned by Spon l. a ruined mosch, this j' imagine was once a christian church raised on the foundation of an ancient temple. near it are the ruins of several ill built habitations, now abandoned wh. we were not permitted to examine, tho' we watched it because the temple of Aglavros seems to have occupied this situation - near that temple likewise stood the

propylaeum, from where there was a shrine called trypod. M the guard house B the upper grand battery n. another gate passing thro which arrive at the top C. the propylea D. the temple of victory without wings (n.b. Stuart it seems places it on the opposite side of Spon & me) E. a high tower, now a prison built on an ancient ruin wh. seems to have been similar to the above described temple. OF another gate - F the Parthenon - G the temple of Erechtheus, Minerva Polias & Pandrosus foundation of an ancient wall, perhaps the pelasgic, it is of hewn stone, well built - H the theatre of Bacchus (this is what I take for the odeum)- II the remains of an ancient portico, perhaps part of the peribolus of the temple of bacchus - K an excavation in form of a theatre, perhaps the odeum - L choragic monument of Thrasylos - above it 2 columns in which tripods have been placed - I a sun dial - qqq this path is probably in the direction of Pausanias' street of the tripods - N grotto at the eastern end of the acropolis - ttt a level space at the foot of the rock where perhaps was another part of the pelasgic wall - V a grotto - n.b. Stuart in his large plan of the parthenon makes the Hypethrial gallery of the larger division go all round but Reveley says that Revett on his second journey to Athens, found that certain ruins had been removed which had previously covered the eastern end of the cell of the temple of Minerva by which means he discovered that the galleries continued on and finished against the eastern and instead of making a return as before supposed, and consequently drawn in Stuart's plan of the temple in his 2nd vol. - Revett found the circle of the two last columns on each side traced on the pavement which was his authority for his opinion.

Again Spon who saw the temple before the fatal bomb says "au dedans du temple on voit tout au tour du rang de colonnes de marbre qui font une manière de galerie, il y en a 23 cm en haut et 22 en bas, parcequ' on n' en a pas mis devant la porte pour ne pas embarasser le passage".

Fauvel is convinced the 2 rows of small columns seen in the inside of the parthenon by Spon, were Greek work of the lower ages the vestiges remaining shew that the pavement had been a little sunk or hollowed to receive their basis - that these had been fixed in it by a pivot - and a channel cut from the outside to this pivot to pour hot lead thro' in order to fix it - things all contrary to the method of the Greeks, in the good time of the arts. Fauvel is positive Stuart was wrong in fixing the grand entrance of the parthenon towards the east instead of towards the propylea F he says the entrance of all great temples was to west - secondly the westerly one is evidently the most enriched and goodly because the castron front still shews in its pediment the remains of the dispute between pallas & neptune described by Pausanias as on the back of the temple. Spon says he saw the parthenon with a double row of columns round the interior of the cella - 23 above and only 22 below parceque on n' en a pas mis devant la porte,

pour ne pas embarasser le passage, now Spon has mistaken on entering the porticus, on the side of the propylea for the pronaos - tho that does not prevent his reason from holding good - Reveley in the preface to Stuart's I vol. says that Revett in a second journey to Athens ascertained that the columns of the hypaethreal galleries ended against the wall on the entrance side and did not return - combining this and Spon's account of the number of columns which perfectly agrees with it from their unknown number, one might make a plan of the parthenon improved on Stuart who has not minded Spon's accurate number of columns".

24. Athens, a general view from the East

Pen drawing on paper 53 × 16cm. Inv. *No* 27231. Inscribed:
"48 - Athènes prise de l' E. I Monument de philopappus. 2 temple de Thesèe".
(Athens from the E. I Monument of Philopappus 2 temple of Theseus).

25. Athens, a partial view with the Acropolis from the South

Pencil drawing on paper 22 × 33cm. Inv. *No* 27234. Inscribed:
"51 - Athènes du midi".
(Athens from the south).

26. View of the Acropolis of Athens

Pen drawing on paper 21.5 × 34cm. Inv. *No* 27233. Inscribed:
"50 - Citadelle d' Athènes".
(Citadel of Athens).

27. Metopes of the Parthenon

Pencil and watercolour drawing on paper 16.5 × 37.5cm. Inv. *No* 27238. Inscribed:
"55 - Bas relief du Temple de Minerve"
(Bas - relief from the Temple of Minerva).

28. Part of the Parthenon frieze - A relief with a Dionysiac scene

Sepia drawing on paper 36 × 49.5cm. Inv. *No* 27154. Inscribed:
"Basrelief of the parthenon, Athens - Basrelief in Signor Logothetis cortile at Athens". This section is from the eastern part of the frieze. The Gods depicted are: Hermes with Dionysus leaning on his shoulder, Demeter and Ares. The standing figure on the left

may be related to the ceremony of the presentation of the peplos which is depicted in vol. V (pl. *No* 29). The relief below, representing Mainads and Satyrs was seen by Hope in the house of Logothetis. Spyros Logothetis, an archon of Athens and the father of the subsequent British vice-consul at Athens, was famous among foreign visitors for his archaeological knowledge and his collection of antiquities. Logothetis' house was situated near the Library of Hadrian; the gateway to its courtyard is still preserved at *No* 14, Areos Street (see: K. Biris, *Athens from the 19th to the 20th C.*, Athens, 1981, in Greek vol. A. p. 19).

29. Athens, a section of the Parthenon frieze

Pen drawing on paper 40 × 60cm. Inv. *No* 27311. Inscribed:
"Bas reliefs in the Acropolis at Athens and group of Caleondgis".
'Caleondgis' are sailors (cf. cat. No 17).
This section of the frieze, which had fallen on to the ground, came originally from the Eastern side of the temple. Seated on the left are the gods Hera and Zeus then follows the ceremony of the presentation of the peplos by the priestess, the archon king and the child with the peplos. Hephaistos is on the right. This entire section of the frieze follows the one which is depicted in pl. *No* 28.

30. Athens, view of the Propylaea from the west

Pen and watercolour drawing on paper 25 × 35cm. Inv. *No* 27237. Inscribed:
"54 - Vue des propylées prise de l' O".
On the *verso* there is the following inscription:
...ΕΝΑΛΕΤΑΝΓΠΙΤΕΣ ΔΙΑΝΤΙΝΟΣ
...ΚΥΣΙΚΕΝΟΗΚΛΑΔΔΕΣΣΕ ΤΙΑΡΙΟΥΤΟΝ ΙΑΝ
...ELLENOTAMIΔΙΣ ΚΑΙ ΠΑΕΔΡΟΙΣ ΔΑΝΕΙΣ
...ΕΛΟΣΑΝΔΟΕΔΟΡΤΑΙΣΕΣΡΑΝΑΘΕΑΝΙΔΑΜΕΜΠΤΟ
...ΣΕΙΚΟΣΑΝΔΟΤΕΙΗΕΜΕΡΑΙΤΕΣΠΡΙΤΑΝΕΙΑΣ
...ΕΠΙΤΕΣΚΕΚΡΟΠΙΔΟΣ ΤΕΤΑΡΤΕΣΠΡΥΤΑΝΕΥΟΣΕΣΔΕ
...ΑΤΕΙΕΥΟΝΥΜΕΙ ΚΑΙΧΡΥΝΑΡΧΟΣΙΣΤΡΑΕΙΘΙΔΙΣΕΔ
...ΕΠΙΤΕΣΑΝΤΙΟΧΙΔΟΣΟΛΔΟΕΣΠΡΥΤΑΝΕΥΟΣΕΣΔΕΧΙ
...ΕΥΟΝΥΜΕΙΚΑΙΧΕΥΝΑΡΧΟΣΙΣΤΡΑΤΙΟΤΑΙΣΕ
...ΕΠΙΤΕΣΑΝΤΙΟΧΙΔΟΣΟΔΔΟΕΣΠΡΥΤΑΝΡΥΟΣΕΣΤΡΙΣ
...ΙΕΥΟΝΙΜΕΙΚΑΙΧΕΥΝΑΡΧΟΣΤΗΝΕΗΟΥΤΟΥΔΕΑΟΣ
...ΕΠΙΤΕΣΑΝΤΙΟΧΙΔΟΣ ΟΛΔΟΕΣ ΠΡΥΤΑΝΕΥΟΣΕΣΕΥΧΟΣ
...ΕΙΕΥΟΝΥΜΕΙΚΑΙΣΙΝΑΡΧΟΣΙΕΣΕΑΝΑΥΣΤΑΕΣΣΙ

...ΕΠΙΤΕΣΑΝΤΙΟΧΙΔΟΣΟΛΔΟΕΣΠΡΥΤΑΝΕΥΟΣΕΣΔΕΥΤΕ
...ΑΡΑΘΩΝΙΟΙΚΑΙΣΤΡΑΤΕΛΟΙΕΝΤΟΙΘΕΜΑΙΡΙΚ...
...ΠΟΙΦΙΔΟΜΕΙΟΙΑΡΑΘΟΝΙΟΚΑΙΣΤΡΤΕΛΟΕΙΝΕΟ
ΚΑΙΦΑΛΑΙΟΝΑΝΑ
ΑΡΧΕΣ....

31-32. Athens, view of the Theatre of Herodes Atticus

Pen drawing on paper 24.5 × 38.5cm. Inv. *No* 27239. Inscribed:
"56 - Vue du Theatre d' Athènes prise du S.E.".
(View of the Theatre of Athens from S.E.).
On the *verso* there is another drawing of the same theatre as seen from the S.E. corner (pl. No 32).

33. Athens, a view with the Pnyx and the mosque of Karà - babà

Pencil drawing on paper 24.5 × 39cm. Inv. *No* 27235 Inscribed:
"52 - Vue de l' Odeum et du Rocher de l' Areopage. 1. Escalier de l' Areopage. 2. Tour moderne 3. tribunal du Pnyx. 4. Coridale. 5. ile Salamine. 6. Moulin moderne. 7. Cimetiere turk dit Cara Baba".
(View of the Odeum and of the Areopagus rock 1. Steps of the Areopagus. 2. contemporary tower. 3. tribunal of the Pnyx. 4. Coridalos. 5. island of Salamis. 6. Contemporary windmill. 7. Turkish cemetery called Cara Baba. For the Turkish cemetery and the mosque of Kara - baba, see: I. N. Travlos, *The Development of the town planning of Athens from Pre-historic ages until the beginning of the 19th C.*, Athens, 1960 (in Greek), p.p - 183-4 - ill. 121.

34. Athens, a view of the Monastery of the Capuchins with the Lysicrates Monument

Pencil drawing on paper 25 × 35cm. Inv. *No* 27240. Inscribed:
"57 - Capuchin Convent Lantern of Demosthenes at Athens".
The same view is depicted in the publication by J. Stuart - N. Revett, *The Antiquities of Athens*, London, 1762 - 1794, 3 vols, Vol. I ch. IV, p. I.

35. Athens, a view with the Olympeion

Pencil drawing on paper 15.5 × 42cm. Inv. *No* 2723. Inscribed:
"53".

36. Athens, a partial view from the South

Pencil and sepia drawing on paper 44 × 16.5cm. Inv. No 27232 Inscribed:
"49 - Athènes prise du S.".
(Athens taken from the S).

37. An ancient rock-cut Tomb on the road to Phaleron

Pencil and pen drawing on paper 17.5 × 23cm. Inv. No 27223. Inscribed:
"40 - tombeau taillé dans le Roc sur le chemin d' Athènes a phalere" (Tomb hewn into the rock on the road from Athens to Phaleron).

38. The coast of Phaleron seen from the West

Pen and sepia drawing on paper 17 × 52cm. Inv. No 27222. Inscribed:
"39 - Vue du port phalero prise de l' 0. - 1. Mont Pentelique - 2. Mont Anchesme - 3. temple de Minerve - 4. monument de Philopappe - 5. mont Hymette".

39. Eleusis, a distant view from the East

Pencil and watercolour drawing on paper 52 × 16.5cm. Inv. No 27244. Inscribed:
"60 - Lefsine (Eleusis) prise de l' E. 1. buste de Ceres 2. isle Salamine 3. ici se voit la mer. 4. Eglise sur les ruines d' un Temple, 5. Caserne 6. ruines ioniques 7. aqueduc".
(Lefsine (Eleusis) taken from the E. 1. bust of ceres 2. island of Salamis 3. here the sea can be seen. 4. Church on the ruins of a temple. 5. Barracks 6. ionic ruins 7. aqueduct).

40. The promontory of Sounion from the North

Pencil and sepia drawing on paper 16.6 × 40cm. Inv. No 27219. Inscribed:
"36 - Vue du Cap Colonne prise du N. - Isle St George d' arbre".
(A view of Cape Colonna from the North - The island of St. George).

41. View of the Temple of Poseidon at Sounion

Pen and watercolour drawing on paper 23.5 × 35cm. Inv. No 27218. Inscribed:
"35 - Vue de temple de Minerve Suniade au Cap Colonne".
The Temple of Poseidon was wrongly attributed to Minerva Sounias until a little before the beginning of the 20th century when an inscription was discovered. Because of the presence of the columns on the edge of the promontory the site came to be called "Cape Colonna".

42. Corinth, view of the Temple of Apollo

Watercolour on paper 23 × 35cm. Inv. No 27245. Inscribed:
"61 - temple de Corinth - n. b. que dans l' original dont j' ai copié ceci les colonnes paroissent encore plus degradés e que partout j' ai mal dessiné la partie au bout des trigliphes sculptée au haut des pierres de l' entablement ou architrave".
(temple of Corinth - n.b. that in the original from which I copied this the columns appear even more worn and that everywhere I have badly drawn the part at the edge of the triglyphs which is sculpted over the stones of the architrave).
Hope refers to the Temple simply as "the temple of Corinth" because the real patronage of the temple was correctly attributed to Apollo only a century later, after the excavations of 1896.

43. Nemea, Temple of Zeus, ground plan

Drawing with pen on paper 16.5 × 24.5cm. Inv. No 27248 Inscribed:
"64".
See: Cat. No 44.

44. Nemea, the Temple of Zeus

Watercolour on paper 23 × 35cm. Inv. No 27247. Inscribed:
"63 - Temple de Nemée - Ce temple est a 5 lieues de Corinth n.b. qué la longueur desproportionée des colonnes n' est pas une faute du dessin mais existe réellement - La fontaine adrastie est a 500 loises de ce monument sur le chemin de Corinthe et yanari".
(Temple of Nemea - This temple is five leagues from Corinth n.b. that the disproportionate length of the columns is not due to a mistake of the drawing but it really exists. The fountain of Adrasteia is 500 loises [?] from this monument on the road between Corinth and Yanari).
For old representations of the temple of Nemea, see:
The Temple of Zeus in Nemea,

45. Mycenae, view of the Citadel

Sepia drawing on paper 19.5 × 29cm. Inv. No 27144. Inscribed:
"Mycenae-platform or esplanade of the citadel-gate of the lions-wall of the cyclops-wall of Agamemnon's tomb-bed of the torrent at the bottom of the precipice wh. separates the esplanade of the citadel from the mountains behind it".
The same view is depicted in vol. V (pl. No 46).

46. Mycenae, a view of the Acropolis

Watercolour on paper 21.5 × 29cm. Inv. *No* 27350. Inscribed: "Mycenae".
The original drawing for this representation is to be found in vol. III, Inv. *No* 27144. (pl. *No* 45).

47. Mycenae, the Lion Gate

Sepia drawing on paper 19.5 × 29cm. Inv. *No* 27149. Inscribed: "Gate of the Lions, Mycenae".

48. Mycenae, The Lion Gate

Sepia drawing on paper 36 × 49.5cm. Inv. *No.* 27152. Inscribed: "Gate of the Cyclops at Mycenae - n. b. the top stone with the Lions measures 10 1/2 ft. in height in the center".

49. Mycenae, The Tholos Tomb or Treasury of Atreus; an outer view

Sepia drawing on paper 19.5 × 29cm. Inv. *No* 2714 . Inscribed: "Treasury of Atreus, Mycenae - part uncovered which serves to light the chambre".

50. Mycenae, The Tholos Tomb or Treasury of Atreus; an outer view

Sepia drawing on paper 19.5 × 29cm. Inv. *No* 27146. Inscribed: "Treasury of Atreus, Mycenae - lowest visible tier of stone".

51. Mycenae, architectural details from the Tholos Tomb or Treasury of Atreus

Sepia drawing on paper 36 × 49.5cm. Inv. *No* 27148. Inscribed: "Details of the Treasury of Atreus, Mycenae - entrance without - entrance within - lateral passage - section of the stone over the entrance on the line a.b."

52. Mycenae, Ground plan of the Tholos Tomb or Treasury of Atreus

Sepia drawing on paper 36 × 49cm. Inv. *No.* 27151. Inscribed: "Plan of the Treasury of Atreus, Mycenae - circumference of the top of the lowest visible tier of stone-circumference at the top of the stone over the entrance-top of the stone over the lateral passage-top of the stone over the entrance".

53. Mycenae, part of the entrance of the so - called Tomb of Klytemnestra

Sepia drawing on paper 19.5 × 29cm. Inv. *No* 27150. Inscribed: "Entrance of the Treasury of Atreus, Mycenae".
Hope identifies the monument incorrectly, in referring to it as The Treasury of Atreus. In fact the tomb depicted here is the other Tholos tomb which is situated on the west side of the Lion Gate and is known as the Tomb of Klytemnestra. This tomb was very little known throughout the years of Turkish domination, which may account for Hope's mistake. G. E. Mylonas in his book *Mycenae Rich in Gold* Athens, 1983, mentions (p. 175): "Tradition has it that its locality was detected during the construction by the villagers of an aqueduct... The channel was accidentally laid across the dome of the tomb; the apex of the dome was struck and the void below it became known... The discovery... probably occurred in 1812". In Hope's drawing we can see in the foreground a kind of channel which is laid near the drum of the tomb. This picture may therefore be one of the earliest representations of this monument.

54. Nafplion, a partial view of the town from the West

Pen and watercolour drawing on paper 17 × 41cm. Inv. *No* 27246. Inscribed: "Naples de Romanie prise de l' 0".
(Napoli di Romania taken from the W.)

55. Nafplion, a general view of the town from the sea

Sepia drawing on paper 40 × 60cm. Inv. *No* 27312. Inscribed: "Nauplia - Palamidi".
See cat. Nos 56-57.

56-57. Nafplion, a general view of the town from the sea

Sepia drawing on paper 40 × 60cm. Inv. *No* 27313. Inscribed: "Nauplia - Palamidi".
This view must have been drawn from the island of Bourdzi because not only is it quite near, but the entire left part of the town can also be seen, whereas in most views it is usually hidden by the Bourdzi fortress. This is a visual record of notable importance for the town of Nauplia in the years before the revolution, because it reveals the town's traditional architectural types. (For other views of Nafplion see: S. Karouzou, *Nafplion*, Athens 1979, in Greek).

58. The Fountain of Hassan Pascha in Nafplion

Sepia drawing on paper 19.5 × 29cm. Inv. *No* 27145. Inscribed:
"Fountain of Hassan Pacha at Nauplia".
The same view is depicted in vol. V (pl. *No* 59).

59. Nafplion, the Fountain of Hassan Pascha

Watercolour on paper 21.5 × 29cm. Inv. *No* 27351. Inscribed:
"Fountain of Hassan Pascha at Nauplia".
The original drawing for this representation is to be found in vol III, Inv. *No* 27145 (pl. *No* 58).
Hassan Pascha was the leader of the Turkish expedition which exterminated the Albanians at Nauplia in 1779.

60-61. Mount Athos, view with the Monastery of Vatopedi

Sepia drawing on paper 42.5 × 64cm. Inv. *No* 27307. Inscribed:
"Mount Athos - Convent of Vatopedi - School of Eugenios".
Surviving representations of Mt Athos are scarce and accidental, because this inaccessible region was not included in the usual itinerary followed by foreign travellers to Greece. The first complete series of views of the monasteries was executed by the Russian monk Basil Grigorovich Barskij (cf N Barsoukov, *Stranstvovanija Vasilija Grigorovica Barskago...*, St. Petersberg, 1885-87, 4 vols), who visited the Holy Mountain in 1725 and 1744.
In this view, the building on the left of the monastery, indicated by Hope as the "School of Eugenios", is of the utmost interest; for it is, in fact, the renowned "Athonias School" which was founded in 1749 by the Patriarch Cyril V and in which the eminent Greek scholar Eugene Voulgaris taught for four years (1749-53). This drawing is the only representation of that building which was erected after Barskij's visit and of which only a few ruins remain today.

62. A male torso from Naxos

Pen drawing on paper 16 × 23cm. Inv. *No* 27214. Inscribed:
"31 - Fragment of a statue at Naxia".

63. A Corinthian capital - A relief

Pen drawing on paper 16 × 23cm. Inv. *No* 27213. Inscribed:
"31 -de pilastre chapiteau corinthien de marbre blanc apartenant a un temple d' Ephese - n.b. comme je l' ai copié d' un pilastre j' aurais du le faire un peu plus large en proportion de sa hauteur, ce qui aurait donné plus de largeur aux feuilles - bas relief in the wall of the Archi episcopal palace at Scyra".
(Corinthian capital of marble belonging to a temple of Ephesus - n.b. as I have copied it from a pillar I should have made it larger in proportion to it height, which would have given a greater width to the leaves).

64-65. See "Introduction", note 3.

66. Aegina, a general view of the city from the North-West

Pen and sepia drawing on paper 17 × 42cm. Inv. *No* 27220. Inscribed:
"Vue de la ville d' Egine - isle d' Egine prise du N.O.".
(A view of the town of Aegina - the island of Aegina from the NW).

67. View of the Temple of Aphaea on Aegina

Pen and sepia drawing on paper 21.5 × 33cm. Inv. *No* 27221. Inscribed:
"38 - Vue du temple de Jupiter panellenien dans l' isle d' Egine prise du S.E.".
(View of the temple of Jupiter Panhellenius on the island of Aegina taken from the SE).
The view that the temple was dedicated to Panhellenius Zeus was universally accepted until the first decade of the 19*th* century, when the question as to who was the real patron of the temple was raised, independently, by the German traveller O. M. von Stackelberg, who excavated there in 1818, and later on by Andreas Moustoxides, the first director of the island's archaeological museum. However, the new attribution was established only after the 20*th* century excavations.

68. View of the Town and Port of Hydra from the sea

Sepia drawing on paper 19.5 × 29cm. Inv. *No* 27142. Inscribed:
"Town and harbour of Hydra".
The same view is depicted in vol. v (pl. *No.* 70).
The indication "a boat" is attached to a rough sketch at the bottom left of the drawing. In the drawing in vol. V this sketch has been completed and three more sailing boats have been added in the foreground.

69. Hydra, a partial view of the Town from a terrace

Sepia drawing on paper 22 × 29.5cm. Inv. *No.* 27143. Inscribed:
"Town of Hydra seen from my Reis's house".
"Reis" means captain of a ship. The same view is depicted in vol. II (pl. *No* 71).

70. Hydra, view of the town from the sea

Watercolour on paper 21.5 × 29cm. Inv. *No* 27348. Inscribed:
"Town of Hydra".
The original drawing for this representation is to be found in vol III, Inv. *No* 27348 (pl. *No* 68).
This and the following view illustrate the island's architecture in a transitional period. We may observe two different types of roofing - one with tiles and the other with a terrace - a feature which may also be observed by the modern visitor. Until the mid eighteenth century travellers to the island mentioned that the houses of Hydra had flat roofs so that the visitor could tour the island by jumping from one roof to another. It seems, however, that around the end of the century, big tile-roofed houses began to appear. These were the properties of the wealthy Hydriote sea-merchants. (For old representations of Hydra, see: R. Malton, *Hydra et la guerre maritime 1821-27*, Athenes, 1953).

71. Hydra, a partial view from the terrace of a house

Watercolour on paper 21.5 × 29cm. Inv. *No* 27349. Inscribed:
"Town of Hydra seen from the platform of my reis's house".
The original drawing for this representation is to be found in vol. III, Inv. *No* 27349 (pl. *No* 69); see also cat. No 69. "Reis" means ship's captain.
This house would be above the church of the Dormition which is built on the wharf. We can easily distinguish its bell-tower which fell and was replaced in 1806 by the one which still stands.

72. Hydra, a view of the harbour

Pencil and watercolour on paper 17.5 × 34cm. Inv. *No* 27250. Inscribed:
"66 - Hydra prise de l' antrée E. du port".
(Hydra taken from the harbour's east entrance).

73. Delos, view from the sea

Sepia drawing on paper 26 × 35cm. Inv. *No* 27211. Inscribed:
"29 - Delos".

74. Myconos, a view from the sea

Sepia drawing on paper 19 × 28cm. Inv. *No* 27136. Inscribed:
"Town of Micony".
The same view is depicted in vol. V (pl. *No* 75), with the addition of boats on the sea.

75. Mykonos, general view of the town from the sea

Watercolour on paper 21.5 × 29cm. Inv. *No* 27347. Inscribed:
"Town of Micony".
The original drawing for this representation is to be found in Vol. II, Inv. *No* 27136 (pl. *No* 74).
This view is of great importance because it shows the island's older architectural style, e.g. a fortified settlement where the facades of the houses create a continuous front like a wall, which affords protection against pirates. It is also a rare visual record as the town of Myconos changed radically soon afterwards, that is from the end of the eighteenth century onwards, when because of the Napoleonic wars the inhabitants acquired wealth which enabled them to build new and bigger houses.(see A Romanos "Mykonos", in: *Greek Traditional Architecture*, vol. 2, Athens, 1982.

76. Tinos, a view of the Town from the sea

Sepia drawing on paper 36 × 49.5cm Inv. *No.* 27140. Inscribed:
"65 - Island and Town of Tino".
The same view with the addition of boats at sea is depicted in vol. V (pl. *No* 77).

77. Tinos, general view of the town from the sea

Watercolour on paper 21.5 × 29cm. Inv. *No* 27347. Inscribed:
"Island and Town of Tinos".
The original drawing for this representation is to be found in vol. II, Inv. *No* 27140 (pl. *No* 76).
Hope's composition shows with particular accuracy the buildings which are, naturally, examples of western architecture since the island was under Frankish domination. Note, for example, the well drawn bell-towers and also the elegant two-storied house

with the loggia, on the left. It is interesting to observe the sea-wall whose purpose was to reinforce the walls of the houses built by the sea.

78. Tinos, the Port of St Nicholas

Pen drawing on paper 15.5 × 44cm. Inv. *No* 27212. Inscribed:
"30 - Port San Nicolo ile de Tine".

79. (See also 86) A Wind-Mill at Paros - A Dove-cote at Tinos

Sepia drawing on paper 21 × 29cm. Inv. *No* 27132 a, b. Inscribed:
"59 - Mill at Paros with 8 wings and little sail between each wing - Pigeon House of Tinos. The lattice work made of bricks".
The same views are also depicted in vol. V (pl. *Nos* 80, 87), the only difference being that human figures have been added there. Hope mistakenly observes that the openings of the Dove-cote were built of brick whilst we know that the islanders used either marble or slate in the construction of the lattices cf. D. Goulandris, *Dove-cotes in Tinos and Andros, Athens,* 1977, with an introduction by T. Charitonidi, (in Greek).

80. A Wind-mill at Paros

Watercolour on paper 19 × 14cm. Inv. *No* 27342. Inscribed:
"Mill at Paros with eight wings and intermediate sails".
The original drawing for this representation is to be found in vol II, Inv. *No* 27132a (pl. *No* 79).

81. Syros, a view from the sea

Sepia drawing on paper 19 × 28cm. Inv. *No* 27135. Inscribed:
"61 - Town of Scyra".
The same view is depicted in vol. V (pl. *No* 82), with the addition of a boat on the left.

82. Syros, view of Ano Syros from the sea

Watercolour on paper 21.5 × 29cm. Inv. *No* 27346. Inscribed:
"Town of Scyra".
The original drawing for this representation is in vol. II Inv. *No* 27136 (pl. *No* 81). Naturally, the view shows only a part of the town, that presently called Ano (upper) Syros. The lower part (e. g. Hermoupolis) was founded later, after the War of Independence. For old representations of Syros, see: I. Travlos - A. Kokkou, *Hermoupolis,* Athens 1980, (in Greek).

83. Antiparos, view of the Grotto

Pen and watercolour drawing on paper 39 × 60cm. Inv. *No* 27310. Inscribed:
"Grotto of Antiparos".
The Grotto of Antiparos was discovered by members of the mission of the French ambassador, the Marquis de Nointel, who travelled in Greece in 1670-80. Nointel recorded in great detail in his diary how the discovery of the grotto was undertaken. (see: N H Omont, *Relation de la visite du marquis de Nointel à la grotte d' Antiparos,* Paris, 1893). Relevant information is also given by a friend of Nointel, the Italina Cornelius Magni, who was an eye-witness and is the author of the publication *Quanto di piu curioso e vago ha potuto raccorre Cornelio Magni..,* Parma, 1679.

84. Paros, a view from the sea

Sepia drawing on paper 21.5 × 29cm. - Inv. *No* 27133. Inscribed:
"View of the Town of Paros".
The same view is alo depicted in vol. V (pl. *No* 85), the only difference being the addition of boats in the foreground.

85. Paros, view of Paroikia

Watercolour on paper 19.5 × 29cm. Inv. *No* 27344. Inscribed:
"Town of Paros".
The original drawing for this representation is to be found in vol II, Inv. *No* 27133 (pl. *No* 84).
Paroikia, the present capital of Paros, is one of the island's oldest settlements.

86. (See No 79.)

87. Dove-cote at Tinos

Watercolour on paper 19 × 14.5cm. Inv. *No* 27343. Inscribed:
"Dove cot at Tino".
The original drawing for this representation is to be found in vol II, Inv. *No* 27132b (pl. *No* 86).

88. Santorini, a view of Scaros

Pencil drawing on paper 25 × 29.5cm. Inv. *No* 27255. Inscribed:

"69 - Santorin, chateau de Scaro vu de l' Est".
(Santorini, the castle of Scaro seen from the East).
Scaros was the strongest of the five medieval fortresses on the island of Santorini. This fortified settlement began to be abandoned early in the 17*th* century when its population moved to Fera. This representation constitutes a unique document as hardly any ruins can be discerned today on the spot and as no other visual record of Scaros is mentioned in the relevant bibliography (cf. D. Phlippidis, "Santorini", in *Greek Traditional Architecture,* vol. I, Athens, 1982, p.p. 147-78). In this drawing every architectural detail has been preserved even that of the drawbridge which blocked the gate of the castle.

89. The Colossus of Naxos

Pencil drawing on paper 16 × 23cm. Inv. *No* 27253. Inscribed:
"68 - colosse non acheué sur la montagne d' apollon a 3 lieues de la ville de Naxia près de la mer a un 1/4 de lieue du village de Comiacki".
(The incomplete colossus on the mountain of Apollo, three leagues from the town of Naxos near the sea, 1/4 league from the village of Komiaki).
The drawing shows the colossal Kouros of Naxos, which still exists in the quarry situated near the bay of Apollo, in the northern part of the island, a short distance from the village of Komiaki.

90. Naxos, view of the town through the Gate of the Archaic Temple

Sepia drawing on paper 43.5 × 29cm. - Inv. *No* 27134. Inscribed:
"60 - Unfinished doorway of a Temple at Paros -
According to Tournefort 18ft high (dans oeuvre)".
The same view is also depicted in vol. V (pl. *Nos* 102).
Hope incorrectly writes "Paros" instead of "Naxos".
The Frenchman Pitton de Tournefort is the author of the traveller's chronicle *Relation d' un voyage du Levant fait par ordre du Roy....,* Paris 1717, 2 vols.

91. Rhodes, a general view of the town

Pen drawing on paper 21 × 27.5cm. Inv. *No* 27257. Inscribed:
"71 - 1. tour de s. angelo 2. interieur du gr. port 3. tour de S. nicolo 4. cimetière hors des murs près la mer 5. partie haute de la ville 6. batteries elevées 7. bout des mats des vaisseaux dans la darse 8. colline eloignée sur laquelle sont partie des faubourgs entremelés de jardins e de palmiers, avec un cimetière au dessous 9. mole ancien qui

forme la darse e communique au chateau St. elme 10. chateau St. elme 11. grouppe de tourbés derriere la darse 12. Moulins qui sont sur le rivage".
(1. tower of S. Angelo 2. interior of the great port 3. tower of S. nicolo 4. cemetery outside the walls by the sea 5. upper part of the city 6. elevated batteries 7. mast tops of vessels in the shipyard 8. distant hill on which are parts of the suburbs intermingled with gardens and palm trees, with a cemetery below 9. ancient mole which forms the shipyard and communicates with the chateau St. Elme 10. Chateau St. Elme 11. group of tourbés behind the shipyard 12. Mills which are on the shore).
This view, in a more condensed form, is depicted in vol V, (pl. No 93).

92-93. Rhodes, a general view from the sea

Sepia drawing on paper 40 × 60cm. Inv. *No* 27314. Inscribed:
"Tower Sant Angelo (fond du grand port) - Tower of San Nicolo - burrying ground outside the walls - highest part of the town - lofty batteries - vessels in the Davia - distant hill covered by a suburb and gardens with burrying ground underneath - ancient mosk closing the Davia and terminates at the castle Sant Elino - group of tumbus behind the Davia, mills on the beach" (cf. pl. *No* 91).

94. Ithaca, a view of Paleokastro

Pencil and watercolour drawing on paper 17 × 35cm. *No* 27297. Inscribed:
"109 - Vue de la montagne paleokastro dans l' isle de Thiaki sur laquelle on pretend que etait le palais d' Ulisse".
(View of the mountain Paleokastro in the island of Thiaki on which the palace of Ulysses is said to have been).
The cone-shaped hills which are here depicted constitute the site which is commonly called Paleokastro or Castle of Ulysses and which forms part of the hilly isthmus which joins the two parts of Ithaca.

95. Zante, a view of the port

Pencil and watercolour drawing 17 × 43cm. Inv. *No* 27295. Inscribed:
"107 - Suite de la Vue de port du Zante prise au milieu du port".
(Continuation of the view of the port of Zante taken from the middle of the port).

96. Corfu, view of the fortress of the port

Pencil and watercolour drawing on paper 17 × 42cm. *No* 27296. Inscribed:

"108 - Vue de Corfou de Coté de l' Est prise en mer".
(View of Corfu from the East taken from the sea).

97. Athens, view of the Theseum from the South

Watercolour drawing on paper 26 × 43.5cm. Inv. *No* 27243.

98. Athens, a view of the Lysicrates Monument

Watercolour on paper 22 × 16cm. Inv. *Vo.* 27241.
(cf. Inv. *No* 27240).

99. Athens, a view of the Lysicrates Monument

Watercolour on paper 22 × 16cm. Inv. *No* 27242.
(cf Cat. No 34).

100. Triumphal monument at Salamis

Watercolour on paper 35.5 × 26.5cm. Inv. *No* 27224. Inscribed:
"Colonne triomphale supposée erigée au cap nord du pirée après la bataille de Salamine - l' original de ce dessin a été restauré par Fauvel d' après les ruines - n.b. les 3oves ne remplissent pas comme elles devraient l' espace entre le volutes et ne s' arrondissent pas assez - ceci represente la mer qui vient frapper le rocher - écume de la mer qui s' éléve".
(Triumphal column that was supposedly errected on the northern promontory of Piraeus after the battle of Salamis - the original of this drawing was restored by Fauvel from the ruins - n.b. the 3 eggs do not fill as they should the space between the volutes and are not properly curved - this represents the sea breaking on the rocks - sea spray).
The monument here may be identified with the so-called Tomb of Themistocles which is situated at Piraeus. According to Hope's note, this monument was already in ruins at the time of his visit and the drawing depicted here was reproduced from Fauvel's imaginary reconstruction. Louis Sebastien Fauvel, the representative of Count Choiseul - Gouffier in Athens from 1780 and the French Consul from 1803, was a well-known collector of antiquities. An amateur painter himself he sketched the antiquities and drew elaborate topographical maps of Athens. (see pl. Nos 22-23).

101. View of the Temple of Apollo Epicurius at Bassae

Watercolour on paper 22.5 × 35cm. Inv. *No* 27249. Inscribed:

"65 - temple dorique dans la morée sur une montagne pres du fleure alphee e de Caritena - n.b. que ce morceau representant une partie de la corniche avec le metope est mal dessiné e devrait etre ainsi-n.b. que l' on apercoit cette echancrure au haut de capelures de tripliphes qui se donnent dans la facade restaurée".
(Doric temple in the Morea on a mountain near the Alpeius river and Karytaina - n.b. that this section which represents a part of the cornice with the metope is badly drawn and should be like that - n.b. that we perceive this excision on the upper part of the triglyphs' channels which look on to the restored facade).
The existence of the celebrated temple of Apollo Epicurius had been forgotten until it was rediscovered in 1715 by the French traveller, J. Bocher. However, it was made broadly known in Europe after the excavations –in 1811 and 1812– by the international treasure - hunting expedition organised by C.R. Cockerell, John Foster, Haller von Hallerstein, the Baron O.M. von Stackelberg, P.O. Bronsted and Georg C. Gropius.

102. Naxos, View of the town as seen through the Gate of the Archaic Temple

Watercolour on paper 44 × 29cm. Inv. *No* 27375. Inscribed:
"Door way of the unfinished temple on the rock at Paros".
The original drawing for this representation is depicted in vol. III, Inv. *No* 27134 (pl. *No* 90). Here, as in the drawing, Hope has mistakenly placed the scene in Paros instead of Naxos. The gate of the archaic temple shown here is still preserved and is called "Portara" (Big Door) by the inhabitants. In Hope's composition this monumental architectural fragment has been used as a pictorial device which dramatically fills the foreground whilst, at the same time, it creates an appropriate frame for the view beyond. With a remarkable economy of means Hope has also succeeded in rendering the dazzling white of the marble as well as the transparency of the atmosphere. All the architectural details of the distant town are thereby brought closer.

103. Rhodes, a view of the old harbour

Watercolour on paper 17.5 × 36.5cm. Inv. *No* 27256.
Here is a view of the fortified old harbour, whose quay walls terminate in two towers. On the left is the tower of St. Nicholas which still exists today. On the right is the tower of De Naillac, named after its founder, Philibert de Naillac, and which fell in 1863. According to C. Karouzos' study, *Rhodes,* Athens, 1949, the two towers were connected by a chain which blocked the entrance to the port. The two turrets on the right of the wall form the double gate of the port, the 'Porta Marina' which still exists today. (For older views of Rhodes, see R. Matton, *Rhodes,* Athens, 1949).

TOPOGRAPHICAL INDEX

(numbers printed in italics refer to Costume drawings)